LIFE IN
ROMAN BRITAIN

ENGLISH HERITAGE
GATEKEEPER SERIES

INTRODUCTION

FOR ALMOST FOUR CENTURIES, much of Britain was part of the enormous, multicultural Roman Empire. During the Roman period a great diversity of exotic visitors came to these shores from all parts of the known world: conquerors, emperors, concubines, slaves, poets, merchants and many more. The people of Britain responded in different ways to contact with the culture of Rome. In the early days there was bloody conflict, as leaders such as Caratacus and Boudicca fought against Roman rule. Although these leaders were defeated, the Empire was unable to pacify the whole of the island. While some British people fought against Rome, others enthusiastically embraced Roman values. They regarded themselves as Romans, dressed appropriately, built themselves Roman-style houses and supported the Roman authorities in the administration of their own tribal people. This book seeks to explore some of the realities and complexities of life in Roman Britain.

The first part of the book looks at the daily experience of the people of Roman Britain. The power of Rome transformed the face of Britain as a network of new roads was built and towns with basilicas and bath-houses were established across the province. The quality of life in Roman Britain depended on one's wealth and status. While the owners of grand town houses and country villas enjoyed lives of considerable opulence, many other people toiled as slaves. The Romans also made their mark on religion in Britain. Many features of earlier Celtic religion were maintained and developed but the mysterious Celtic priesthood of the druids was destroyed.

In the second and third parts of the book the relationship between Britain and the wider Empire is considered. What was it like to be a Roman soldier in Britain, or the wife of an officer posted to Britain? Extraordinary archaeological evidence, such as the collection of military documents and letters found at Vindolanda, provides a window into this strange world. We see senior officers using their time in Britain as a stage in a glittering career. On a more mundane level, we also see soldiers ordering socks and underpants to help them cope with the rigours of the British climate.

Although Britain was always a remote part of the great Empire, it was on occasion the setting for high imperial politics. We see, for example, the Emperor Claudius arriving in Colchester with elephants as he tried to outdo the achievements of Julius Caesar. Two centuries later, the Emperor Severus and his wife come to Britain hoping, in vain, to tame their wild and murderous sons.

The last part of the book deals with the end of Roman control and the heritage of the Romans. During much of the fourth century, there were few signs of imminent collapse; the great Emperor Constantine came to power in Britain, the Empire became Christian and the rural villas of southern Britain enjoyed their finest hour. The end came suddenly in the early fifth century when, faced by problems in Gaul and Italy, the imperial authorities were unable to offer adequate protection to Britain.

Although the Roman period came to an abrupt end, the legacy of the Romans lives on and is evident in such diverse fields as language, politics, law and religion. The achievements of Roman times can also be appreciated by visitors to the many Roman sites in the care of English Heritage and others.

MAIN PICTURE *A reconstruction drawing of Great Witcombe villa in Gloucestershire. This magnificent country house nestled at the foot of the Cotswolds. Like many villas it was located a short distance from urban amenities available in the nearby town of Gloucester*

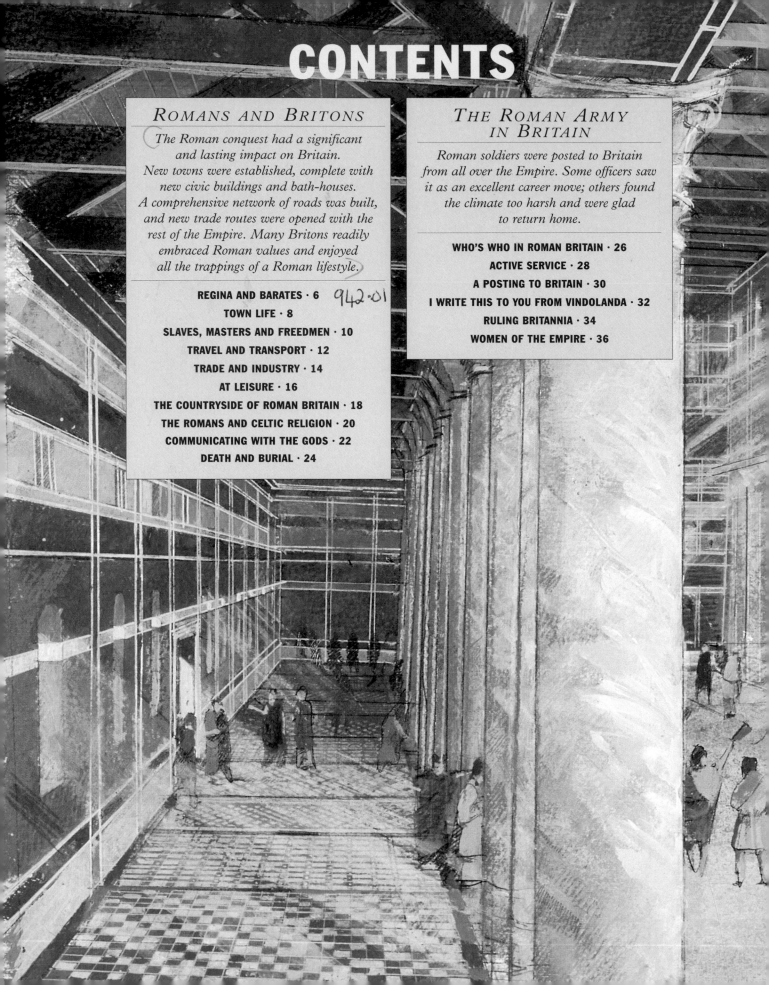

CONTENTS

ROMANS AND BRITONS

*The Roman conquest had a significant
and lasting impact on Britain.
New towns were established, complete with
new civic buildings and bath-houses.
A comprehensive network of roads was built,
and new trade routes were opened with the
rest of the Empire. Many Britons readily
embraced Roman values and enjoyed
all the trappings of a Roman lifestyle.*

REGINA AND BARATES · 6

TOWN LIFE · 8

SLAVES, MASTERS AND FREEDMEN · 10

TRAVEL AND TRANSPORT · 12

TRADE AND INDUSTRY · 14

AT LEISURE · 16

THE COUNTRYSIDE OF ROMAN BRITAIN · 18

THE ROMANS AND CELTIC RELIGION · 20

COMMUNICATING WITH THE GODS · 22

DEATH AND BURIAL · 24

THE ROMAN ARMY IN BRITAIN

*Roman soldiers were posted to Britain
from all over the Empire. Some officers saw
it as an excellent career move; others found
the climate too harsh and were glad
to return home.*

WHO'S WHO IN ROMAN BRITAIN · 26

ACTIVE SERVICE · 28

A POSTING TO BRITAIN · 30

I WRITE THIS TO YOU FROM VINDOLANDA · 32

RULING BRITANNIA · 34

WOMEN OF THE EMPIRE · 36

942·01

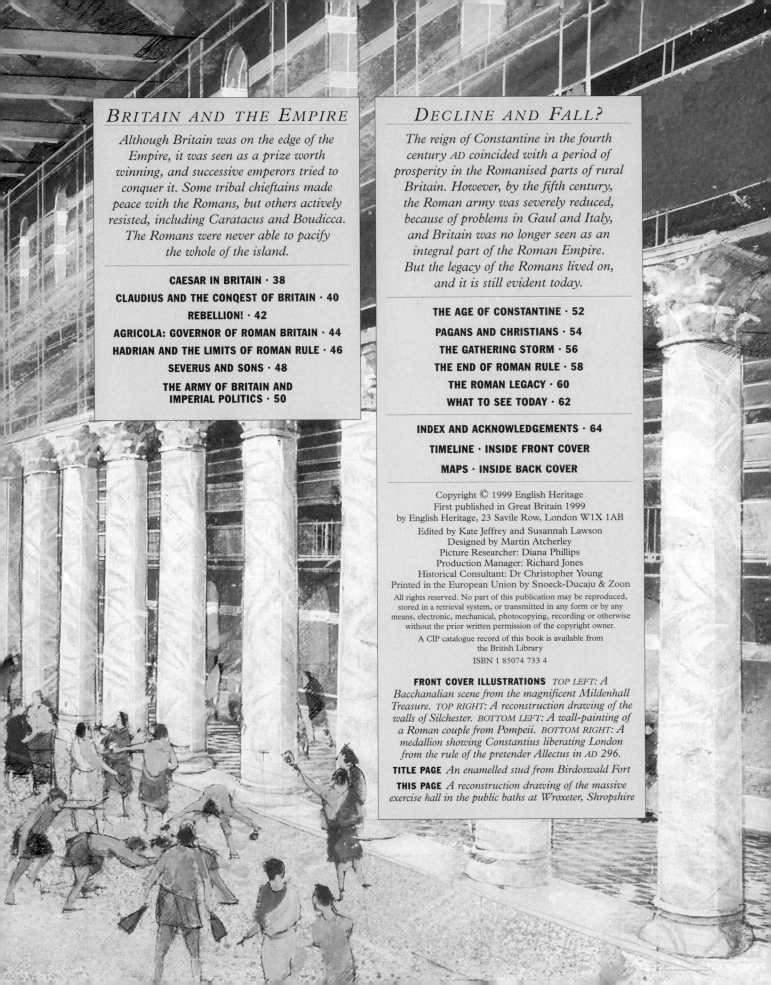

BRITAIN AND THE EMPIRE

Although Britain was on the edge of the Empire, it was seen as a prize worth winning, and successive emperors tried to conquer it. Some tribal chieftains made peace with the Romans, but others actively resisted, including Caratacus and Boudicca. The Romans were never able to pacify the whole of the island.

CAESAR IN BRITAIN · 38

CLAUDIUS AND THE CONQEST OF BRITAIN · 40

REBELLION! · 42

AGRICOLA: GOVERNOR OF ROMAN BRITAIN · 44

HADRIAN AND THE LIMITS OF ROMAN RULE · 46

SEVERUS AND SONS · 48

THE ARMY OF BRITAIN AND IMPERIAL POLITICS · 50

DECLINE AND FALL?

The reign of Constantine in the fourth century AD coincided with a period of prosperity in the Romanised parts of rural Britain. However, by the fifth century, the Roman army was severely reduced, because of problems in Gaul and Italy, and Britain was no longer seen as an integral part of the Roman Empire. But the legacy of the Romans lived on, and it is still evident today.

THE AGE OF CONSTANTINE · 52

PAGANS AND CHRISTIANS · 54

THE GATHERING STORM · 56

THE END OF ROMAN RULE · 58

THE ROMAN LEGACY · 60

WHAT TO SEE TODAY · 62

INDEX AND ACKNOWLEDGEMENTS · 64

TIMELINE · INSIDE FRONT COVER

MAPS · INSIDE BACK COVER

Copyright © 1999 English Heritage
First published in Great Britain 1999
by English Heritage, 23 Savile Row, London W1X 1AB

Edited by Kate Jeffrey and Susannah Lawson
Designed by Martin Atcherley
Picture Researcher: Diana Phillips
Production Manager: Richard Jones
Historical Consultant: Dr Christopher Young
Printed in the European Union by Snoeck-Ducaju & Zoon

A CIP catalogue record of this book is available from the British Library

ISBN 1 85074 733 4

FRONT COVER ILLUSTRATIONS *TOP LEFT: A Bacchanalian scene from the magnificent Mildenhall Treasure. TOP RIGHT: A reconstruction drawing of the walls of Silchester. BOTTOM LEFT: A wall-painting of a Roman couple from Pompeii. BOTTOM RIGHT: A medallion showing Constantius liberating London from the rule of the pretender Allectus in AD 296.*

TITLE PAGE *An enamelled stud from Birdoswald Fort*

THIS PAGE *A reconstruction drawing of the massive exercise hall in the public baths at Wroxeter, Shropshire*

ROMANS AND BRITONS

The Roman conquest had a significant and lasting impact on Britain. New towns were established, complete with new civic buildings and bath-houses. A comprehensive network of roads was built, and new trade routes were opened with the rest of the Empire. Many Britons readily embraced Roman values and enjoyed all the trappings of a Roman lifestyle.

REGINA AND BARATES

The arrival of Roman power in Britain led to a remarkable meeting and mingling of cultures. Two tombstones found in the north-east of England commemorate a husband and wife who died in the area, probably in the late second century. They were called Regina and Barates, and they symbolise the cosmopolitan nature of life in Roman Britain. From the inscriptions on their tombstones we can piece together two extraordinary lives, shaped by the strange realities of life in Roman Britain.

Barates originated thousands of miles away from Britain, in Palmyra, an important city in Syria. He might have been a merchant who traded in military flags and ensigns. He was presumably drawn to Britain and the Hadrian's Wall area because of the large number of soldiers based there. The lavish nature of his wife's tombstone suggests that Barates was a successful merchant. There are also other indicators of wealth and status: Regina is depicted with a casket by her side, on which is a crescent decoration and a substantial lock. This was used to store her personal collection of jewellery, several pieces of which she is wearing.

The journey of Barates from Syria to Britain illustrates the cosmopolitan nature of the Roman Empire. Doubtless many other traders were attracted to Britain by the spending power of the large garrison on this frontier of the Empire. The units of the Roman army with which Barates did business were themselves linked to places far from Britain. Auxiliary units on Hadrian's Wall included, for example, Pannonians (from modern Hungary) and Thracians (from modern Bulgaria). These units had originated in the regions after which they were named, although by the time of Barates much of the recruitment probably took place in Britain. Barates and Regina appear to have lived in the South Shields area. We know that a unit of Tigris barge-men was based in South Shields at a later period. The River Tigris (in modern Iraq) is even further away from South Shields than Barates' home town of Palmyra.

Unlike Barates, Regina was a native of Britain. Her tombstone states that she was a member of the Catuvellaunian tribe, who lived in the south of England, in the region of modern St Albans. Tribal groupings, such as the Catuvellaunians, were an important feature of Roman Britain.

Regina is described on her tombstone as the wife and freedwoman of Barates. A freedman or freedwoman was a former slave, and it seems that Regina was the slave of Barates before he freed her and married her. Like many of her contemporaries, she died young, at the age of only thirty. Barates himself was more fortunate and lived to the age of sixty-eight.

The idea of slavery is repugnant to us today but it was a common feature of Roman life and of all ancient societies. Barates was able to buy Regina after his arrival in Britain, so there was clearly a functioning market in slaves. How did young Regina come to be a slave? Some were enslaved as

ABOVE *Barates is commemorated on this tombstone. He was clearly fond of his young British wife and former slave*

ABOVE *Celtic gold torcs. Regina is shown wearing a torc on her tombstone*

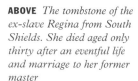

ABOVE *The tombstone of the ex-slave Regina from South Shields. She died aged only thirty after an eventful life and marriage to her former master*

result of warfare and conquest, others were the children of slaves, but neither of these are likely explanations in the case of Regina. Scholars believe that she might well have been sold into slavery by her parents. We know that this was not unusual in other parts of the Roman Empire. Attitudes towards men and women were very different in Antiquity and perhaps a daughter was seen as less of an asset than a son.

Barates gave Regina her freedom in a process known as 'manumission', which was very common. It was not however, about whether Regina really wanted to marry Barates, or whether she reluctantly agreed to marry him in order to end her slavery. It does seem that Barates was fond of his British wife and former slave. Her elaborate tombstone must have cost a lot of money. In addition to a Latin inscription there is a very unusual phrase in Palmyrene, Barates' native tongue that says, 'Regina, the freedwoman of Barates, alas!'

Regina straddled two different

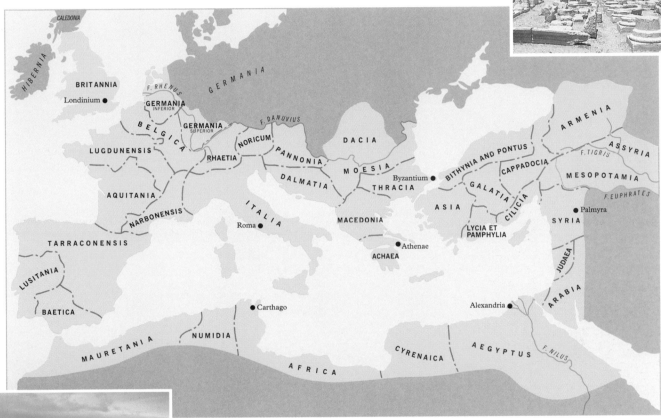

unusual for a master to free a female slave in order to marry her. The *Digest*, a great summary of Roman law, laid down rules governing such matters. It stated that if a man gave a slave woman her freedom on condition that she marry him, then she had no right to go back on her word and the wedding must take place. This was apparently intended to stop slave women from promising marriage and then reneging once free. It is not possible to say with any certainty how the couple felt about each other. One can speculate, cultures, and her tombstone reflects this, as she is depicted as both a respectable Roman lady and a member of a Celtic tribe. She is remembered in a Latin inscription, but one that describes her as 'of the Catuvellaunian race'. Her dress is a so-called 'Gallic coat', a large tunic that was worn throughout the north-western provinces of the Empire, yet round her neck she wears the distinctive Celtic solid neck-ring, known as a torc – symbolic of power and status in the Celtic world. With her torc and her Classical tombstone, Regina, former slave and merchant's wife, embodies some of the remarkable changes that took place in Britain during the Roman period.

TOWN LIFE

ABOVE *A Roman barrel*

Romans considered towns and cities to be a vital feature of a mature society. Once conquered, Britain was divided into a series of city-states, known as 'civitates', roughly based on pre-conquest tribal areas. In each tribal territory a central town was developed or established. The town and its dependent territory constituted the key unit of Roman local government in Britain. These towns were also equipped with a number of public buildings that symbolised the Roman way of life:

◆ A public bath-house
◆ A basilica for meetings, trials and other official business
◆ A forum for trade and as a meeting place
◆ Sometimes an amphitheatre for sports, and more rarely a theatre for drama and religious ritual

The Roman governing class saw the development of town life as a means of integrating a newly conquered province. Tacitus famously described how Agricola, as governor of Britain, used civic amenities in British towns as a successful instrument of Romanisation:

> His object was to accustom them to a life of peace and quiet by the provision of amenities. He therefore gave private encouragement and official assistance to the building of temples, public squares and good houses… And so the population was gradually led into the demoralising temptations of arcades, baths and sumptuous banquets. The unsuspecting Britons spoke of such novelties as 'civilisation', when in fact they were only a feature of their enslavement.
> *(Tacitus, early second century AD)*

Each tribal area in Roman Britain had a council which met at the principal town of the region, the 'civitas capital'. Membership of the council was restricted to men of the landowning class, known as 'decurions' or 'curiales'. The minimum age for membership was usually thirty. These councils were miniaturised local versions of the senate which met in Rome to discuss the affairs of the Empire. Decurions were responsible for the collection of imperial taxes. This could be an onerous

responsibility because they were obliged to make up any shortfall. Another burdensome aspect of council membership was an expectation that major public projects in towns would be paid for by individual local magistrates. Little evidence has survived of such patronage in Britain. One exception is the theatre at the small town of Brough-on-Humber (known to the Romans as 'Petuaria') where, in about AD 140, a rich decurion called Marcus Ulpius Januarius proudly commemorated his own generosity:

> For the Honour of the Divine House of the Emperor Antoninus Pius, father of his country, three times Consul, and to the deities of the Emperors, Marcus Ulpius Januarius, magistrate of the community of Petuaria, presented this new stage building at his own expense.

A number of cities, such as Colchester, Gloucester and Lincoln, had a special status because they were founded as 'coloniae', privileged settlements for veteran soldiers and their families. A legionary fortress at Colchester was converted into a major Roman-style town, with a population of retired veteran legionaries in AD 47. Colchester was intended to demonstrate the nature and benefits of Roman rule to the people of Britain. It was given distinctive Roman buildings, including a 'senate house' or council chamber, a theatre and a huge Classical temple. The significance of Colchester was clearly evident to British people, and not all of them were pleased by what they saw. One of the first acts of the British rebels, led by Boudicca in AD 60, was to attack Colchester and destroy all the Roman civic buildings. The Roman historian, Tacitus, recounted how the rebels made a special point of attacking Colchester because they saw it as the 'citadel of their servitude'.

Some mystery surrounds the origins of London, the greatest city of Roman Britain. There is no evidence that it

ABOVE *Grand town houses were decorated with elaborate murals such as this second-century AD wall-painting from London*

ABOVE *The exercise yard at Wroxeter as it might have looked in about AD 150. Notice the outdoor pool*

BELOW *The greatest town of Roman Britain was London. Archaeologists have discovered much fascinating Roman material beneath modern London, such this oil lamp in the shape of a sandalled foot from the Jubilee Line excavations*

was deliberately established as either a 'civitas capital' or a 'colonia'. Tacitus described London at the time of the revolt of Boudicca as 'a town which, while not distinguished by the title of colony, was a very important and busy centre for traders and goods'. It appears to have developed around a river crossing at an important junction in the Roman road network. The town was devastated by the rebels in AD 60 and largely rebuilt. The face of London changed dramatically between AD 90 and 120, as it was ambitiously transformed into the capital of the province of Britannia. It was given an enormous new forum and basilica, a new amphitheatre and two bath-houses. The main hall of the basilica (on the site of Leadenhall Court, in the middle of the modern city of London) was an extraordinary 150 metres long (500 feet). A substantial fort was built at Cripplegate, close to the amphitheatre so that the troops could use it for training and

the city authorities built walls as a symbol of civic pride and that there was competition between towns for the most impressive walls.

Some towns have been explored in more detail than others by archaeologists. One place that has been the focus for many modern excavations is Wroxeter in Shropshire. It was the 'civitas capital' for the Cornovii people of modern Shropshire and Cheshire. Originally a legionary fortress, Wroxeter was handed over to the local people after the departure of the legions. The excavation of the forum has shown that it was once the site of a bustling market, as artefacts from all over the Empire have been found. Excavation revealed stacks of unbroken Gaulish Samian ware abandoned during a fire at the forum in about AD 170. The basilica formed part of the forum complex: this was where the local magistrates held trials and where the provincial governor would sit in justice

ABOVE *A reconstruction drawing of the walls of Silchester. At first Roman towns were undefended*

drill. The fort had a complement of 1000 men, seconded from the province's legions to provide a household force for the governor of the province. The scale of the building work of AD 90–120 clearly marked London out as the leading town of the province.

The first towns of Roman Britain were largely unfortified. Many towns were defended in the second and third centuries. At first these defences were generally earth ramparts, which were later replaced in stone. In London, for example, a three-kilometre-long wall was built between AD 190 and 220, and the line of this wall continues to have an important influence on the layout of the modern city. The reason for building these walls is not clear. It does not seem to be linked to any particular military threat. One explanation is that

during his visits. The trials took place in the tribunal, a raised area at one end of the basilica. It seems likely that business deals and meetings took place in the rest of the basilica hall.

The houses of the wealthier residents of Wroxeter included high-status features, such as wall-paintings, hypocausts (underfloor heating) and bath suites. One house, which presumably belonged to a leading member of the Cornovii tribe, had over twenty-five rooms, a veranda and a fine view. The local élite appears to have enjoyed the trappings of a Roman-style existence. Not every aspect of Romanisation was completely successful. An outdoor swimming-pool was built as part of the bath-house complex that was established in about AD 150 but it was abandoned after about fifty years.

ABOVE *A busy street scene in the small town of Wall. This settlement grew up alongside a major Roman road*

BELOW *This leather shoe was found at Old Penrith*

SLAVES, MASTERS AND FREEDMEN

ABOVE *Some slaves were born in Britain, others originated from other parts of the Empire. This slave was called Victor the Moor and presumably came from north Africa. He was freed by his former master, a cavalryman*

Slavery was universal in the Ancient world. Educated Romans took it for granted that the conquest of a new province, such as Britain, would yield a harvest of slaves. At the time of Julius Caesar's expeditions to Britain, the Roman orator Cicero wrote to a friend, dismissively commenting that the only likely benefit would be the acquisition of unskilled slaves:

> It has also become clear that there isn't an ounce of silver in the island, nor any prospect of booty except slaves. I don't suppose you're expecting any of them to be accomplished in literature or music!

A letter found from Roman London indicates that there was a slave market in the city. A man called Rufus wrote to a servant with business instructions including an order to arrange the sale of a slave:

> Rufus, son of Callisunus, greetings to Epillicus and all his fellows. I believe you know I am very well. If you have made the list, please send. Be sure that you look after everything carefully. See that you turn the slave girl into cash.

Life was doubtless very hard for many slaves. In Roman law, slaves were not people with rights, but objects whose owners had rights. We have little evidence for the treatment of slaves in Britain, but we do know from other parts of the Empire that they could be treated brutally. Conditions were particularly bad for some slaves working on farms and in the mines. Domestic slaves could also be treated with routine violence. The poet Martial described as something commonplace the way a master would beat a slave whose cooking was not up to scratch:

> You say that your rabbit has not been cooked well and you call for your whip. You prefer to cut up your cook, rather than your rabbit.
> *(Martial, late first century AD)*

Letters that have recently been

LEFT *Slaves were valuable property and could be hunted down if they absconded. This bronze slave tag from Italy says 'Hold me lest I flee and return me to my master'*

discovered at Vindolanda, a fort on Hadrian's Wall, show that slaves played an important part in the life of a military unit in Roman Britain. Officers at Vindolanda had their own personal slaves. In the letters, the officers refer to their slaves as their 'pueri' or 'boys'. Cerialis, the officer at Vindolanda, had a slave called Privatus who regularly purchased foodstuffs for the commander's household. There were special purchases for festivals, including the acquisition of wine for 'the festival of the goddess'. Intriguingly, there is a letter between two slaves, Candidus and Severus, who write to each other to discuss arrangements for the Saturnalia. This festival to the god Saturn was held on 17 December and was the one day of the year when slaves were not expected to work. Traditionally, on the Saturnalia, roles were reversed and slaves were served by their masters.

BELOW *A black slave cleaning a boot*

While the lives of many slaves were bleak, it would be quite wrong to think that all slaves were treated in the same way. Some enjoyed a relatively high status. One example is a man called Anencletus, who was described on his wife's tombstone as a 'slave of the province'. This meant that he was, in effect, a senior civil servant, working for the provincial council based in London. The word Anencletus is Greek and means 'blameless'. His elevated position in society is indicated by the quality of the expensive monument to his wife and the fact that his wife was a free woman.

On occasion, male owners had children with the slave women of their household. A tombstone at Chester appears to commemorate the 'vernae' or slave children of one Pompeius Optatus. The inscription is an early one and may date from about the time that the garrison arrived at Chester and Optatus was probably a soldier. A number of tombstones refer to 'alumni' which means foster-children or foundlings. There are many possible reasons that could explain someone being described as an 'alumnus'. One possibility is that they were abandoned children who were rescued and brought up as slaves.

Many slaves were fortunate enough to be freed after a period of substantial service. The usual minimum age for freedom or 'manumission' was thirty. Former slaves were known as 'freedmen' and 'freedwomen' and they continued to have a legal relationship with their former owner after manumission. The links between freedmen and their former owners are clear from inscriptions and monuments. We know, for example, of two freedmen called Eutuches and Lemnus from Bath. They set up altars to the local goddess Sulis, calling for the health and safety of their patron and former owner, M. Aufidius Maximus, centurion of the Sixth Legion. There is evidence of a tightly-knit group of freedmen, freedwomen and slaves from Chester. The 'freedmen and slaves of the household' of Pomponius Mamilianus were responsible for a religious dedication. Their master, Mamilianus, was the commanding officer of the Twentieth Legion, based in Chester.

ABOVE *It was expected that slaves, when freed, would continue to have a relationship with their former owners. This Italian tombstone was erected in honour of a married couple by their ex-slaves*

The most powerful former slaves were the imperial freedmen. They were, in effect, senior civil servants. An imperial freedman called Marcio served for a while in the administration of Britain. He was in Britain during the middle of his career and he had an extraordinarily varied life. We know some of his life story from an inscription found in Phrygia, in modern Turkey, where he also served. Before coming to Britain he ran the imperial marble quarries, and he later took charge of the scenery at theatres in Rome. Another imperial freedman, Polyclitus, was sent by the emperor to investigate a dispute at the top level of the administration of Britain in the first century AD. Tacitus described how Polyclitus travelled in great state from Rome to Britain with an enormous entourage. Such was the power of Polyclitus that Tacitus referred to him as 'an object of dread'.

ABOVE *Some freedmen prospered. This tombstone shows a former slave, on the right, in business as a manufacturer and retailer of knives*

LEFT *A slave with a serving tray. The experiences of slaves in the Roman world were extremely varied*

TRAVEL AND TRANSPORT

ABOVE *An axle cover of leaded bronze showing a lion mask, from Lullingstone Villa, Kent*

BELOW *A Roman haulier transports wine. His cart is pulled by oxen and his dog relaxes on the wine barrels*

The Romans were famous for the quality of their straight, metalled roads. These roads usually ignored local contours and land-ownership patterns and covered the shortest distance between any two points. Road-engineering was the responsibility of the legions. They began by laying down a deep and solid foundation of layered broken stone. Above the foundations were placed further layers of finer stone, rammed earth or gravel and a hard, smooth cobbled surface. Roads were given a gentle camber, or arch, and the cobbles were closely fitted to prevent the penetration of rain-water. Under Roman law, maintenance work on the roads was the responsibility of local administrations, and labouring on the roads could be given as a punishment for some crimes. So, as in some parts of the United States of America today, one might have seen chain-gangs of criminals at work as one travelled along the roads of Roman Britain.

Although roads were useful to British civilians and traders, the main purpose of the Roman road system was the smooth-running of the Empire. The imperial government relied upon the road system both as a means of moving military forces rapidly from place to place, and as a way of quickly communicating governmental information and decisions.

The imperial post was known as the 'cursus publicus'. The main roads of the Empire were covered with regular post-houses, at intervals of about fifteen miles, with more elaborate inns placed about thirty miles apart. The so-called *Antonine Itinerary* lists 200 routes and stopping places of the 'cursus publicus' in the early third century. It gives fifteen routes through Britain, such as a journey from London to Caerleon in Wales in three days via Silchester and Bath. The system was developed by the Emperor Augustus. His biographer Suetonius said that Augustus wanted a single messenger to be able to carry a message rapidly across the Empire in person so that questions could be asked and views sought at the other end. At the official inns or 'mansiones', official travellers could obtain fresh horses and a bed for the night. Messengers routinely travelled an impressive fifty miles a day. When the Emperor Claudius came to Britain to oversee the invasion of the island he travelled the 540 miles

BOTTOM *A reconstruction drawing showing Wall in Staffordshire. This bustling settlement developed alongside a Roman road*

BELOW *The extant Roman road in Wheeldale, North Yorkshire. The road system was constructed by the legions for military and administrative reasons*

ABOVE *An altar of Yorkshire millstone grit taken from York to Bordeaux. Such a long journey by boat could be extremely hazardous and needed divine protection*

from Marseilles to Boulogne in ten days. Faster journeys were possible; the Emperor Tiberius famously once travelled 200 miles in twenty-four hours. Some of the post-houses and inns developed into more substantial settlements; the small town of Wall in Staffordshire is thought to have begun life as an inn on the 'cursus publicus'. One fourth-century writer described how the future emperor Constantine made his way to Britain along the 'cursus publicus', killing the horses at the post-houses as he went along, so that his enemies would not be able to follow and apprehend him:

> Having killed the post-horses along his route in order to frustrate those pursuing him, he reached Britain. For he was being held as hostage by Galerius. Just at that time death was pressing hard upon his father Constantius.
> *(Aurelius Victor, fourth century AD)*

While navigable rivers were often used for bulk transportation, roads were used to transport an extraordinary diversity of goods across the Empire. One indicator of the efficiency of the Roman road system is the frequency with which oyster shells are found at Roman sites, because fresh oysters have a limited life. They were either moved at great speed along the roads of Britain or there was a sophisticated system for the transportation of heavy water tanks containing the oysters. Ox-drawn wagons were used for heavy freight. There are references to the haulage business in the Vindolanda letters that date from about AD 100. In one letter the writer asks that a consignment of lime should be dispatched urgently:

> I ask you to order them to be loaded without pause so that they make their way to us early in the morning.

In another letter, probably written in January, one Octavius comments on the problems associated with moving a wagon of hides in winter:

> I would have already been to collect them except that I did not care to injure the animals while the roads are bad.

Travel by sea was greatly feared by the Romans. It was considered an act of daring for the Emperor Constans, one of Constantine's sons, to cross the Channel (or 'Ocean' as the Romans called it) in the middle of winter, early in AD 343. One sycophantic writer celebrated this act in fulsome terms:

> You, Constans, you have changed and scorned the order of the seasons, trampling underfoot the swelling, raging waves of Ocean in winter time, a deed unprecedented in the past, and not to be matched in the future. Beneath your oars trembled the waves of a sea still scarcely known, and the Briton trembled before the face of an emperor he did not expect.
> *(Julius Firmicus Maternus, fourth century AD)*

An altar set up at Bordeaux in AD 237 provides further evidence of the Roman fear of sailing. It was set up in gratitude to the gods for a safe journey from York to Bordeaux by one Marcus Aurelius Lunaris. The altar was made of Yorkshire gritstone and was apparently taken by Lunaris on his long journey.

Despite these concerns about safety, there was a well-organised system of international sea transportation. An analysis of some of the building stone used in London, for example, reveals several cases of stone from the eastern Mediterranean being shipped to Britain. On a more day-to-day level, massive quantities of pottery were routinely brought from Gaul to Britain.

BELOW *The Roman lighthouse can still be seen at Dover in the grounds of the later medieval castle*

Much of the cross-Channel trade went through the port of London with Boulogne as the most common destination at the other end. London was both the centre of the road network and the busiest port of the province. Wrecks of Roman merchant ships have been discovered in the Thames. Storage jars of the first and second centuries have been excavated from the Pudding Lane area of the city, indicating a very substantial level of imports of olive oil, wine and fish sauce. Excavations have also revealed an elaborate system of waterfront warehouses and a possible customs house dating to the early second century AD.

ABOVE *We know that there was considerable trade in luxury goods between Britain and the Continent. This sculpture shows a Roman wine merchant's ship, with its oarsmen and cargo*

TRADE AND INDUSTRY

ABOVE *A shopkeeper sells fruit and vegetables from his trestle table*

ABOVE *A steelyard weight in the form of a satyr, from Richborough*

There was trade between Britain and the Roman world long before the island became part of the Empire. In the early first century Hengistbury Head in Dorset was regularly visited by merchants from Gaul. Italian amphorae, glass and metalwork have been found on the site, together with Gaulish pottery. We also know that Cornish tin was exported in the first century BC:

> Those inhabitants of Britain around the promontory called Belerium (Land's End) are particularly hospitable and civilised in their way of life as a result of their dealings with foreign merchants. They it is who produce the tin, working the ground that bears it in an ingenious way. They mine the ore and refine it by smelting. They hammer it into the shape of knucklebones and transport it to an island that lies off Britain called Ictis [possibly St Michael's Mount]. There, merchants buy the tin from the natives and transport it to Gaul. Finally, making their way through Gaul for around thirty days, they bring their merchandise on horseback to the mouth of the river Rhone.
> *(Diodorus Siculus, late first century BC)*

Julius Caesar said that before his invasion, the only visitors to Britain were merchants. Once conquered, Britain provided many opportunities for merchants, not least the business of supplying the great army of occupation. Some foreign traders probably accompanied army units when they travelled to Britain. This might have been the case with Salmanes, a man whose name is recorded on an inscription in Scotland near the Antonine Wall at Auchendavy. Salmanes is a Syrian name, and it is clear from the inscription that he was not a soldier, though a Syrian unit, the Hamian Archers was based at Auchendavy. If Syrian merchants in Scotland were comparatively rare, foreign merchants would have been a very familiar sight on the waterfront in London. The tombstone of a man from Athens, called Aufidius Olussa, has been discovered in London, where he died at the age of seventy; as with Salmanes, the absence of reference to a military background leads one to assume that he was a merchant.

Amphorae are sometimes inscribed with a reference to their contents. One amphora, for example, that has been discovered in London bears the words 'Lucius Tettius Africanus – finest fish sauce from Antipolis'. This shows that the fish sauce in question had come all the way from Antibes in the south of France. We also know from continental sources about some of the people who made their living through commerce with Britain. Trade with the Rhineland was substantial, and an inscription from Cologne describes one C. Aurelius Verus as a 'shipper in the British trade'. A statuette from Lancaster bears the name of its maker, Servandus of Cologne. On the Rhine at Kastel, near Mainz, is an inscription referring to Fufidius, 'a merchant from Britain'. We also know that there was significant trade with Bordeaux, where a 'merchant dealing with Britain' called Secundinus, is recorded on a tombstone.

There was a long tradition of extracting and working metal in Britain before the advent of Rome. After the Roman conquest the imperial authorities took a particular interest in the mining of metals. The invading force immediately

ABOVE *This lid of a lead container is evidence for trade in medicinal herbs. It was found in Germany and its inscription suggests that it contained an item known as 'the British root'*

ABOVE *An amphora containing fish paste imported from Gaul*

set about exploiting the resources of the new province. Lead mines at Charterhouse in the Mendips appear to have been operational as early as about AD 50. A significant settlement grew up around the lead mine, including a small amphitheatre. There was an important gold mine at Dolaucothi in south Wales and a fort was located close by to guard and oversee the work of the mine. There was also state involvement in the iron industry. The most important centres for the mining and processing of iron were the Forest of Dean and the Weald in Kent and Sussex. In the Weald it seems that the British fleet of the Roman navy – the 'Classis Britannica', based at Dover – was directly involved in the organisation of the industry. By the second century AD, Roman Britain was self-sufficient in the production of iron and there might have been substantial exporting of British iron.

RIGHT *Samian ware pottery, imported in large quantities from the Continent*

BELOW *Glassware of the first century AD found in Buckinghamshire*

Enormous quantities of pottery have survived since Roman times. The market was supplied both by potters in Britain and imported pottery. The most famous of the imported pottery types is the so-called 'Samian ware', a glossy red decorated tableware, which was manufactured in north-east Gaul and the Rhineland. British potters also operated on a commercial basis, and the names of over 250 potters from Roman Britain are known. Most of them inscribed their own names, presumably as a form of advertising, on large mixing-bowls known as 'mortaria'.

As today, plans for new enterprises were not always successful. We know that about 160 potters from east Gaul set up in Colchester to make Samian-style pottery, as traces of 400 of their moulds have been excavated. However, few examples of their work are known outside the Colchester area, and unfired pots discovered at the site suggest that the enterprise came to a sudden and abrupt ending.

The production of Samian pottery in Gaul went into decline after about AD 200. British potters sought to fill the gap in the market and the potters of the Nene Valley area were particularly successful. The Nene Valley pottery industry was based around the small town of Water Newton near Peterborough, known to the Romans as Durobrivae. The Nene Valley potters were well situated close to Ermine Street for transport to London. The River Nene was used to take pots to the North Sea for coastal transport both north and south. Substantial houses hint at the profits that were made by the owners of the Nene Valley potteries, although money from ceramics was probably only one component in their wealth.

Roman Britain exported goods to the rest of the Empire. Woollen rugs and a woollen coat, similar to a duffle coat, were distinctive British products. (The coat was known as a 'Birrus Britannicus'.) Nemesianus, writing in the third century AD, said, 'Britain sends us swift hounds, adapted to hunting.' In AD 400, Claudian noted that, 'British beer is worthy of mention.' The value of British beer was also recognised by a specific mention of the product in the Empire-wide edict on prices, proclaimed by the Emperor Diocletian in AD 301. Diocletian attempted to fix the price of British beer at twice the price of Egyptian beer; this presumably indicated its greater desirability.

ABOVE *A bronze steelyard with a lead weight discovered at Gestingthorpe, Essex. Marks for calibration are visible on the bar*

LEFT *These cloaked gods from Housesteads show some of the garments made in Roman Britain*

AT LEISURE

HUNTING

As in many other periods of history, the wealthier country dwellers of Roman Britain were keen on hunting. Even before the arrival of the Romans, Britain was renowned for the quality of its hunting dogs. A mosaic from a villa at East Coker in Somerset celebrates the chase and shows men carrying a deer home after a successful hunt. Some animals were evidently taken alive; the poet Martial referred to Caledonian bears being captured and sent to Italy to die in the Roman amphitheatres. We also know that senior army officers enjoyed hunting. The documents found at Vindolanda include a note from the commander of the fort to a close friend, calling for hunting equipment:

> Flavius Cerialis to his Brocchus, greetings. If you love me brother, I ask that you send me some hunting-nets.

This letter dates from about AD 100. In the third century AD, an altar dedication from Stanhope in Weardale describes the hunting prowess of an equestrian officer in boastful terms:

> Gaius Tetius Veturius Micianus, prefect of the Sebosian cavalry regiment, on fulfilment of his vow willingly set up this for taking a wild boar of remarkable fineness which many of his predecessors had been unable to bag.

BATHING

Bathing was a very popular activity throughout the Roman Empire. In the largest rural villas of Britain, rich people often had their own bath suites. In major towns, people of all backgrounds had the opportunity to go bathing in the public bath-houses. There were nominal charges for bathing but children, soldiers and slaves were let in for free. Emperor Hadrian tried to forbid mixed bathing, and in the largest baths there were separate male and female bath suites. In the smaller baths, there were usually different opening times for men and women. Baths were not just for bathing; they were used for a range of fitness activities, such as ball-games, running and athletics, and massage. Some, such as the celebrated baths at Bath, were also religious centres. Seneca the Younger gave a very lively account of the realities of a public bath-house:

ABOVE *A mosaic showing sea creatures. The houses of the wealthy were lavishly decorated*

> I live above a public bath. I can hear all sorts of irritating noises. There are groans when the muscle-men are exercising with their weights. Some unfit men just have a massage and I hear the slap of hands beating their bodies. Ball-players come along and shout out the score in their match. Drunks have arguments, thieves shout when they are caught, some men sing in the baths. People dive into the pool with a great splash. There are shouts from those selling drinks and snacks.
> *(Seneca the Younger, first century AD)*

Excavations at the baths at Caerleon in Wales have confirmed some aspects of Seneca's account. Archaeologists have discovered evidence of the consumption of substantial amounts of shellfish by users of the baths. These cooked 'fast-food' snacks included mussels, whelks and other more exotic shellfish.

THE THEATRE

Some towns in Roman Britain had theatres, although Britain did not have as many as the Mediterranean provinces. Theatres were used for drama and religious ritual. A magnificent ivory carving of an actor's tragic mask has been found at Caerleon.

found on pottery vessels, glassware, mosaics and statuettes. A pot discovered at Colchester shows several named gladiators fighting each other and wild animals. An intact gladiator's helmet, found at Hawkedon in Suffolk, might have been used in the amphitheatre at nearby Colchester.

There are some clues suggesting that Roman-style leisure activities attracted only limited support in Britain. Several important towns, including Silchester and Wroxeter, do not appear to have had a theatre. Before the end of the fourth century AD, the theatre at Verulamium (modern St Albans) was abandoned and became a rubbish dump. The history of bath-houses provides a similar pattern. The story of the baths at Exeter hints at local uncertainty about the merits of Roman-style bathing. In Exeter the legionaries built a large bath-house very early on, with a full suite of rooms. The importance of bathing to the soldiers is indicated by the fact that the baths were the only substantial stone building in the fortress. In about AD 85 the legionaries left Exeter and the fortress was handed over to become the new 'civitas capital' for the tribe of the Dumnonii. Strangely, one of the first acts of the new owners was to demolish the bath-house and establish the forum and basilica on its site. It does not seem that bathing was a high priority for the people of Exeter.

ABOVE *Two bone dice from Wall*

We know the name of one actress from Roman Britain: inscribed on a pot found in Leicester are graffiti immortalising an actress called Verecunda and her boyfriend, Lucius, who was a gladiator. Theatres could accommodate large crowds: the one at Canterbury had a capacity of about 7000, so that almost the whole population of the town could have attended a single event.

GLADIATORS

The sites of amphitheatres are known in eight towns in Britain. These arenas had a number of functions: military training, gladiatorial combat, baiting and killing animals and executing criminals. Some archaeological finds hint at the popularity of gladiatorial combat in Britain. A number of depictions of gladiators have been

ABOVE *An ivory carving from Caerleon of an actor's mask*

LEFT *This pot from Colchester shows particular named gladiators at work. Here we see Memno with his helmet and sword. His opponent has lost his weapons and can only raise his finger to Memno*

THE COUNTRYSIDE OF ROMAN BRITAIN

ABOVE *Most inhabitants of Roman Britain lived in the countryside. This reconstruction drawing shows rural life just outside the walls of the Roman town of Silchester*

ABOVE *Views of a plough-share excavated at Gestingthorpe, Essex. This type of plough-share first appeared in Britain during the Roman period*

Much of Britain had been extensively farmed long before the Roman conquest. The analysis of pollen samples from archaeological sites shows that most woodland had been cleared in southern Britain many centuries earlier. Iron Age farmers appear to have been efficient and there were important technical innovations during the first century BC, such as the use of drainage ditches to improve the productivity of fields.

The Romans soon learned that while there was fertile farming land in Britain, it was not possible to produce many of the crops grown in the Mediterranean lands. The historian Tacitus was told about the British weather, and its impact on agriculture, by his father-in-law, Agricola, who was a first-century governor of Britain:

> The climate is wretched with its frequent rains and mists, but there is no extreme cold… The soil will produce good crops, except olives, vines and other plants which usually grow in warmer lands.

The thorough exploitation of the countryside continued during the Roman period. New varieties of wheat were introduced and new culinary herbs were grown, such as coriander and dill. The study of bones on excavated sites suggests that large numbers of cattle, sheep and pigs were kept. Pork was particularly popular among the military.

The Roman authorities were keen to exploit the economic potential of their provinces and there is evidence that Roman Britain exported significant amounts of food. One Roman writer described Britain as:

> A land so rich in harvests, with such abundant pasture a lucrative source of so much tribute, girded round with so many ports, so vast in its extent. *(Panegyric to Constantius, AD 297).*

Another writer explained how exported wheat was taken via the River Rhine, until barbarian attacks disrupted the trade:

> In earlier times corn was shipped from Britain, first over the sea and then up the Rhine, but since the barbarians had become a force to be reckoned with, they had blocked its transport and the cargo vessels had long since been dragged ashore and had rotted away. A few still plied, but since they discharged their cargo in coastal ports, it was necessary to transport the grain by wagon instead of by river, and this was a very expensive affair. *(Libanius, fourth century AD)*

There was a significant difference between the countryside of the south-eastern half of Britannia and the north-western region. In the south-east, Roman-style country houses known

ABOVE *A ploughman at work. This bronze figurine was found at Piercebridge, County Durham*

BELOW *Circular 'Celtic' homesteads. Most inhabitants of the Roman countryside lived not in villas but in traditional houses such as this*

as villas were established, and many of these were the centres of rural estates. With their bath-houses, mosaics and underfloor heating, the largest villas were ostentatious stone-built structures that announced to the world the wealth of their owners and their allegiance to a Roman lifestyle. In the north and west of Britain, few villas have been found, and farming centred on native homesteads. We tend to associate the Roman countryside with villas. However, the great majority of country-dwellers lived not in villas, but in houses built in the style of the pre-Roman Iron Age. These 'native' houses were usually circular in plan, and made of timber and thatch. One archaeologist has calculated that only one per cent of people in Roman Britain lived in villas.

ABOVE *A seated landowner checks his tenants' accounts*

BELOW *A reconstruction drawing of Great Witcombe villa. The owner of the villa might well have been a prominent figure in the nearby town of Gloucester*

The advent of the Romans brought both changes and continuity to the countryside. In contrast with the later Saxon and Norman settlements, there is no evidence that the British aristocracy was substantially dispossessed of its lands. The landowners of Roman times were, for the most part, descended from the people of Iron Age Britain. Power, social status and land ownership went together, and prestigious posts in local government could only be held by those who owned sufficient land. Villas were often located close to towns and it seems likely that the wealthy men who controlled the towns liked to ride out to their elaborate country houses.

Excavations at Lullingstone villa in Kent have provided us with a vivid picture of the lifestyle of the wealthier country dwellers under Roman rule. A small stone villa was built in the second century, on the site of an earlier timber house. A suite of baths was added later in the century, with a sequence of hot, tepid and cold baths. Bathing was a social activity and eventually a large cold plunge bath was installed so that about six people could bathe simultaneously. This bath leaked and had to be repaired on several occasions. Like many villas, Lullingstone enjoyed a period of great prosperity in the first half of the fourth century AD. At this time the dining-room was extended and decorated with a magnificent new mosaic – a depiction of a scene from Virgil, showing Jupiter disguised as a bull abducting Europa. We know that the prosperous fourth-century owners of the villa were Christian because traces of a lavishly decorated chapel have been discovered at the site.

ABOVE *A mosaic from Lullingstone Roman Villa showing Jupiter in the form of a bull abducting Europa*

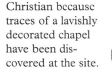

LEFT *A bronze figure of a goddess. There is substantial evidence of pagan and Christian belief in the countryside of Roman Britain*

THE ROMANS AND CELTIC RELIGION

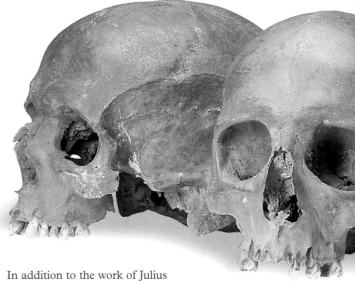

ABOVE *This striking Celtic stone is topped with a human head framed by two snakes. The human head seems to have played an important part in Celtic belief and ritual*

TOP *This eighteenth-century painting by Noel Halle of a druid's ceremony shows the participants dressed in long flowing robes. It is unlikely that druids in Roman Britain really looked like this*

The Romans were generally tolerant of the different beliefs of their subject people. They maintained and developed many of the cults that Celtic people practised in Britain before the Roman conquest. One exception to this pattern of tolerance was the Roman attitude to the priestly class known as the druids. We tend to think of druids as being dressed in long white robes, but this is a modern preconception, largely based on ideas developed less than 200 years ago. Roman literature suggests that the druids were a powerful priestly class among the Celtic people of Gaul. The evidence for a similar situation in Britain is much less substantial. Julius Caesar said, 'The druidic religion is thought to have been found in existence in Britain and taken from there to Gaul. Nowadays those who study it deeply still go to Britain.' Roman references to the druids in Gaul were often hostile. The historian Diodorus Siculus gave a typically negative and colourful account of the druids and other Celtic priests:

When enquiring into matters of real import they have a strange and incredible custom; they put to death a human being and stab him with a dagger in the region above the diaphragm, and when he has fallen they foretell the future from his fall, and from the convulsions of his limbs and, moreover, from the spurting of the blood.
(Diodorus Siculus, first century BC)

In addition to the work of Julius Caesar, there is only one other major literary source for the history of the druids in Britain. The Roman historian Tacitus described in some detail their role in the battle for Anglesey in AD 60. This graphic account is worth quoting in full:

Along the shore stood the enemy in a close-packed array of armed men interspersed with women dressed like Furies in funereal black, with streaming hair and brandishing torches. Round about were the Druids, their hands raised to heaven, pouring out dire curses. The Roman troops were so struck with dismay at this weird sight that they became rooted to the spot as though their limbs were paralysed and laid themselves open to wounds. Then, bolstered by the encouragements of their commander and urging one another not to be afraid of this mass of fanatical women, they advanced with their standards, cut down all they met, and enveloped them in the flames of their own torches. After this a garrison was imposed on the conquered natives, and the groves devoted to their savage rites cut down; for it was part of their religion to drench their altars with the blood of captives and to consult their gods by means of human entrails. *(Tacitus)*

This passage seems straight-forward enough: the druids were powerful magicians who incited

ABOVE *A collection of first-century human skulls from the Wallbrook in London from the Roman period*

BELOW *A dark side of Celtic belief is hinted at by the discovery of Lindow Man in Cheshire. This body, dating from about the first century AD, appears to have been a human sacrifice*

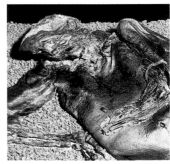

the Britons to resist the Romans, and their religion involved human sacrifice. Scholars, however, have their doubts about what Tacitus had to say. He described events in AD 60, almost thirty years after the arrival of the Romans. No other Roman writers mention the druids in their accounts of the early decades of Roman rule. If the druids were so powerful, it is strange that they are ot mentioned prior to the events of AD 60. Tacitus made much of their bloodthirsty penchant for human sacrifice. It is possible that this was simply anti-British propaganda.

If the druids are a mystery, what do we know about religion in Britain at the time of the coming of the Romans? The Celts believed that there was a sacred quality to much of the natural world and, in particular, they revered natural sources of fresh water. Archaeological evidence shows that ritual offerings were often placed in wells, springs and rivers – a tradition that continued into Roman times. It seems that fresh water was seen as a boundary and connection between this world and the supernatural world.

Some springs were also considered to have magical healing powers. We know that Celtic sacred springs, such as Bath and Coventina's Well on Hadrian's Wall, flourished under Roman rule.

Another major cult centre dedicated to the worship of a Celtic god, Nodens, was based at Lydney in Gloucestershire. Lydney is close to the estuary of the River Severn and Nodens appears to have been a god with aquatic connections: sea monsters and depictions of fish have been found on many objects at the site, as well as a large number of representations of dogs (in the Classical world, dogs were often associated with healing cults). In Ancient Greece we know that live dogs were kept at healing centres and were thought to have magical powers of healing if they licked the sick part of the pilgrim's body – perhaps this also happened at Lydney. There was a complex of buildings around the temple of Nodens: a guesthouse for visiting worshippers, a temple, a bath suite and a mysterious long, narrow building. This is thought by many scholars to be an 'abaton', a familiar feature of many Roman and Greek ritual healing centres; it was a sacred dormitory, where worshippers hoped that they would be visited by the resident deity in their sleep and their affliction cured.

ABOVE Both Celts and Romans revered sacred springs such as this one at Bath

ABOVE A cult image from a temple at Benwell on Hadrian's Wall. It represents the local Celtic god, Antenociticus

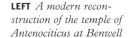

LEFT A modern reconstruction of the temple of Antenociticus at Benwell

COMMUNICATING WITH THE GODS

ABOVE *A reconstruction drawing of the main cult statue of Mercury at the temple at Uley in Gloucestershire*

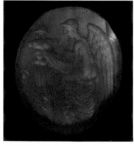

ABOVE *An inscribed gem stone from Lullingstone Villa showing the goddess of Victory*

RIGHT *The god Mithras slaying a bull. The cult of Mithras was male-only and was popular among some soldiers*

Celtic and Roman religious life was much concerned with ways of contacting the gods in order to predict and influence the future. These beliefs still influence our language today: the word 'auspicious' comes literally from a Latin word meaning 'bird watching', because one form of divination in Rome itself was to study and interpret the flight patterns and eating habits of birds, which were seen as messages from the gods. Throughout the Empire, a common way of communicating with the gods was through the sacrifice of live animals. The level of sacrifice at some sites was enormous: at Uley temple in Gloucestershire 150,000 animal bones have been excavated. The nature of the sacrificial animals varied from place to place. At Uley there was a preponderance of bones from male goats and male fowl: the goat and the cockerel played a major part in the worship of Mercury, the Uley deity. We know from depictions of scenes of sacrifice that the ritual was accompanied by the burning of incense and the playing of music, which might have drowned out any ill-omened cries from the animals. Afterwards there was usually a feast involving the consumption of the sacrificial meat. Sacrifice at a major temple would be a well-organised process, with a number of specialist contributors.

At important cult sites the liver of a sacrificed animal was very carefully removed and examined by a specialist fortune-teller known as a 'haruspex' (the word literally means 'gut-gazer'). At Bath, in 1965, archaeologists came across the base of a statue, very close to the site of the sacrificial altar, that was inscribed with the name of one of the sacrificial fortune-tellers: 'To the goddess Sulis, Lucius Marcius Memor, Haruspex, gave this gift.' This dedication indicates the importance of the religious complex at Bath. A haruspex was only to be found at major sacrificial sites and was a very distinguished official. The great sacrificial altar at Bath, where Lucius Marcius Memor worked, was

ABOVE *This fragment of the large cult statue of Mercury from Uley was discovered in a modern excavation*

LEFT *A gilt bronze figure of Mercury from near Hadrian's Wall*

an imposing structure. It was in the open air, set within a courtyard next to the main temple building. It was about 1.5 metres high and almost 2.5 metres wide. Over the years, three of the four large decorated corner blocks have been discovered, including one built into the fabric of a medieval church at Compton Dando thirteen kilometres from Bath.

The religious complex at Bath was built on the site of an earlier cult centre. The worship of Sulis at Bath was organised in a typically efficient manner during the Roman period. A third of a million gallons of mineral water was produced a day by the sacred spring at Bath. Romans implemented a well-planned system of drainage to organise this great mass of water. Excess water is still carried away today by the great drain built during the Roman period. Such is the size of this drain that a human could easily walk inside it. A series of manholes was placed at street level so that the drain could be maintained. An enormous lead-lined tank was built above the spring to channel water off from this reservoir to the baths. At first the tank was open and worshippers would have gazed in wonder at the huge amount of magical, hot, bubbling water that emerged. The reservoir was rendered more mysterious and sacred by changes in the late second century AD, when it was covered over, and access to the sacred spring was restricted. Visitors admired the waters through three large windows and threw offerings to the deity.

Part of the deposit of offerings to the sacred spring was excavated between 1979 and 1980. The archaeologists found a huge number of offerings, including thousands of coins and many cups and pots inscribed with dedications to Sulis Minerva. Strange offerings included a representation of female breasts carved from elephant ivory. It was common for ill people to leave at such a site a representation of the part of the body for which they sought some relief. Many curses were written on pewter and thrown into the spring by people seeking the support of the goddess. On one curse, a man named Annianus asks Sulis for help in the recovery of six silver pieces that had been stolen, mentioning eighteen suspects by name.

Curse tablets, inscribed on thin sheets of lead, have been found at a

LEFT *The Emperor Marcus Aurelius conducts a sacrifice. Such rituals were a major feature of Roman religion*

ABOVE *A depiction of a sun god from Corbridge*

ABOVE *This mysterious male gorgon's head dominated the entrance to the temple at Bath. Gorgons were thought to ward off evil spirits*

number of other sacred sites. Supplicants made their complaint to the resident deity and asked for help. The majority of these complaints refer to theft and suggest that petty crime was very common in Roman Britain. The following is an example of a typical curse tablet from the temple at Uley, which was dedicated to Mercury:

> Honoratus to the holy god Mercury. I complain to your divinity that I have lost two wheels and four cows and many small belongings from my house. I would ask the genius of your divinity that you do not allow health to the person who has done me wrong, nor allow him to lie or sit or drink or eat, whether the thief is man or woman, whether boy or girl, whether slave or free, unless he brings my property to me.

The tradition of giving valued items to the gods was well-established in pre-Roman Iron Age Britain: coins, weapons and jewellery are often found at sacred sites. Coins and jewellery are also found on sites dating to the Roman era but by Roman times civilian weapons were banned by law and disappear as a votive offering. Under Roman rule objects were manufactured specifically for votive use. Almost certainly many ritual sites attracted traders with kiosks selling these votive objects and other religious trinkets. These items included miniature weapons, such as tiny axes and spears and also miniature figurines of the gods.

DEATH AND BURIAL

The study of tombstones excavated at cemeteries provides us with substantial information about life and death in Roman Britain. Tombstones may not be typical, but they suggest that there was a very high death rate among young children and that men, on average, lived longer than women. This pattern is also evident from the analysis of actual human remains. At Cirencester, for example, a study of 300 skeletons pointed to a life-expectancy of about forty-one years for men and thirty-seven for women. The longer life-expectancy of men is, of course, the reverse of the modern pattern and is probably a consequence of the risks of dying in childbirth. Despite the probability of dying young, there were people who lived to enjoy considerable old age. At the legionary fortress of Caerleon in Wales, Julius Valens, a veteran of the Second Legion, was commemorated by his wife after dying at the age of a hundred.

Phrases used on tombstones followed standard formulae and were the work of professional funerary sculptors. Nevertheless, it is still possible to get some sense of the grief felt by the bereaved of Roman Britain from the inscriptions on tombstones. At Risingham a man called Dionysius Fortunatus put up a tombstone for 'his most devoted mother'. His message, which is found on other tombstones, was, 'May the earth lie light upon thee'. Quintus Fortis, the father of a girl called Corellia who died at the age of thirteen, was apparently devastated by his loss and had little faith in an afterlife:

> After the brief light of life, I, the father of an innocent daughter, a pitiable victim of unfair hope, lament this, her final end.

During the first two centuries of Roman rule, cremation was the most popular way in which the bodies of the dead were disposed of. Inhumation – the burial of the whole unburnt body – became increasingly common in the later Roman period. Roman cemeteries were, by law, placed outside the boundaries of the town. Cemeteries were usually sited alongside the main roads out of a town. Only new-born babies could be buried within a town and any other bodies found within a Roman settlement can be assumed to be the victims of foul play.

It was widely believed that the correct rituals must be followed for burial, otherwise a spirit could not rest in peace. Roman citizens looked to their families to ensure a proper burial. For the poorest in society, including slaves, families could not necessarily provide, and such people formed burial clubs for mutual support. The tombstone of a slave called Hardalio, found near Hadrian's Wall, was paid for by a club of fellow-slaves. The regulations of a similar slaves' funeral club has survived from a small Italian town:

> If any member has not paid his fair share for six months, and meets death, arrangements will not be made for his funeral. For any member of this club that has paid his dues regularly and then dies, 300 sesterces will be allotted from the club treasury for his funeral…. If any member of this club who was a slave should die, and if his body should not be handed over to us for interment because of the unfairness of his master or mistress, a funeral will be held for an effigy of him.
> *(Constitution of a funeral club, AD 133)*

It was customary in the Roman Empire for dead bodies to be washed, dressed and taken at night to a cemetery, followed by a formal procession of mourners. At the cemetery, speeches were made celebrating the memory of the deceased. If the body was to be cremated this took place close to the grave; at one cemetery near York, ashes and scorching indicate the place where bodies were usually burnt. Traditionally, a banquet was held at the the side of the grave, and mourners returned annually for further commemorative banquets. Burial ritual also entailed the pouring of votive drinks or libations. A trace of these customs remained at

ABOVE *A fragment of an altar from Old Penrith. Sacrifice was an important part of funerary ritual*

ABOVE *The tombstone of one Julia Velva from York with her son and other members of her household. Inscriptions on tombstones often describe the grief felt by bereaved relatives*

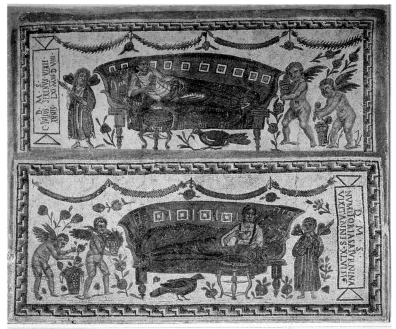

Caerleon in Wales, where cremation burials were found to be linked to the surface by a tube, so that ritual drinks could be poured down by mourners above.

There was some diversity of funerary practice in Roman Britain. Some people were buried with grave goods, others with very few objects. Where grave goods are present they were intended to help the deceased in the next life. There are often traces of a meal for the spirit of the deceased: meat, eggs and a drink. A common find in inhumation cemeteries are hobnails from leather shoes or boots; it seems that bodies were shod with special footwear to help them on their journey. In cemeteries near York and Dorchester, liquid gypsum was poured into coffins to help to preserve the bodies of the dead for future resurrection. The preservative powers of the gypsum were such that the hair of the dead sometimes survived until its discovery by modern excavators. Sometimes a coin was placed in the mouth of the deceased to pay the customary toll to Charon, the ferryman of the Underworld.

There are indications in burial practice of differences of social class. High-ranking people were sometimes interred inside little enclosures or mausolea. While some bodies were simply placed in the ground, others rested in wooden or lead coffins. At a Colchester cemetery the bodies were placed in wooden coffins wearing shrouds. Remarkably, one of the shrouds appears to have been made of Chinese silk.

Some of the strangest and most mysterious of customs relate to the treatment of the head after death. At several cemeteries bodies were decapitated and the heads were placed between the legs of the deceased. At Wroxeter pieces of human skull were found, covered with vegetable oil after the skin from the heads had been removed. One head shows evidence of scalping; another had been kept on a bronze plate and the bronze had stained the bottom of the skull green. During the early second century AD, decapitated male heads were thrown into a tributary of the Thames in London. The skulls appear to have been placed in the open air before they were thrown into the stream (see photograph on page 20).

THE ROMAN ARMY IN BRITAIN

*Roman soldiers were posted to Britain from all over the Empire.
Some officers saw it as an excellent career move; others found
the climate too harsh and were glad to return home.*

WHO'S WHO IN ROMAN BRITAIN

During the first two centuries of Roman rule, Britain was administered as a single province of the Empire. The **governor** of Britain was always a high-ranking senator by background. He controlled the army and much of the civil administration of the province. The governor was also the most senior judge in Britain.

Taxation and the finances of the province were administered by a high official called the **procurator** who reported separately to the emperor. There was often tension between the procurator and the governor. The actions of a money-grabbing procurator called Decianus Catus were one of the causes of the revolt of Boudicca.

Each legion of the Roman army was commanded by a **legionary legate**. This could be an important post for an ambitious 'senatorial' Roman. One of the early legionary legates in Britain called Vespasian went on to

BELOW *Roman officers depicted on a hunting scene on the side of a sarcofagus*

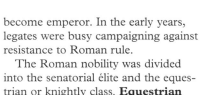

ABOVE *A second-century statuette of a legionary*

become emperor. In the early years, legates were busy campaigning against resistance to Roman rule.

The Roman nobility was divided into the senatorial élite and the equestrian or knightly class. **Equestrian officers** were given important commissions in the Roman army. They commanded the auxiliary regiments and they also held senior posts in the legions. During the first two centuries of Roman rule there were about sixty equestrian officers in Britain at any one time. The writer Suetonius was offered a position as an equestrian officer in Britain but he declined and the post was given to one of his relatives called Silvanus.

Senatorial and equestrian Romans typically joined the army for a brief period early in their careers. In contrast, **legionary centurions** were career soldiers. One centurion who served in Britain, called Petronius Fortunatus, was in the army in total for an amazing fifty years. Each legionary centurion was in charge of a 'century', a group of eighty men (originally a century had a strength of a hundred but by the time of the Empire the number had been reduced). The chief legionary was known as the 'primus pilus' which means 'number one javelin'; he was a very powerful man. Under the Emperor Trajan the 'primus pilus' was paid four times as much as the ordinary centurion.

Legionaries were élite infantry soldiers and Roman citizens. After the first century AD, three legions were based in Britain at Caerleon, Chester and York, where they served for twenty-five years. We know the names of many individual legionaries from their tombstones. One legionary from Caerleon called Tadius Exuperatus was commemorated by his mother and sister; his inscription describes how he died 'on the German expedition'. Tombstones from Chester indicate that some men had joined the legions young; two men had been only fourteen when they had joined up.

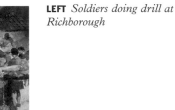

LEFT *Soldiers doing drill at Richborough*

Auxiliaries played a central part in the British garrison. In the early days they were often recruited from border provinces of the Empire. Auxiliary units were either cavalry or infantry, or a mixture of both, and they included some specialists, such as the Syrian archers who served in Britain. Cavalrymen in the auxiliary units were better paid than their infantry counterparts and they are recorded on far more surviving tombstones; a massive tombstone of a trooper called Flavinus, for example, was found at Hexham Abbey where it had been reused by medieval builders. After twenty-five years service the auxiliaries were rewarded with Roman citizenship.

Retired soldiers were known as **veterans**. They were a group with enviable legal privileges, including exemption from taxation. Some were settled in special towns known as 'coloniae'; the Roman authorities liked the idea of loyal ex-soldiers living together. Legionaries were given a large discharge grant when they retired. Possibly the earliest record of veterans in Britain is the tombstone of a legionary veteran called Antigonus who died aged forty-five. Perhaps he retired to Bath in the hope of a cure for his medical problems.

Roman **merchants** were in contact with Britain before the conquest and more merchants followed the soldiers into the new province. These merchants were a cosmopolitan group. We know of one man called Diogenes from an inscription in York, who was from central Gaul and his wife, Julia Fortunata, who was Sardinian. Diogenes was probably on business, trading between northern Britain and the Rhineland. Another merchant, one Aurelius Verus, is described on an inscription found at Cologne as 'a shipper in the British trade'.

ABOVE *Officers were supported by large numbers of servants such as this cupbearer*

ACTIVE SERVICE

ABOVE *A stamped tile showing the boar, symbol of the Twentieth Legion, which was based in Chester*

BELOW *Legionaries in battle, first century AD. They were highly trained and disciplined infantry troops*

Britain became part of the Roman Empire in AD 43 when the forces of the Emperor Claudius invaded the island. While the Romans established themselves in south-east Britain, attempts to conquer and control the whole of the country led to several decades of fierce fighting. These efforts at complete conquest did not succeed and only the southern half of the island was permanently brought under Roman rule. As a result of the failure to subdue the northern tribes, a large garrison was permanently stationed in Britain.

What was it like to be a soldier on active service in Roman Britain? A soldier's lot depended, amongst other things, on whether one was a member of the élite legions or the second-class auxiliary units. The legionaries were recruited from Roman citizens, whereas the auxiliaries were not. Legionary soldiers had more status and better conditions of service. In the early second century AD, for example, legionaries were paid three times the wages of auxiliary infantrymen. On retirement, legionaries received a substantial severance pay, equivalent to fourteen years salary; auxiliaries were rewarded with Roman citizenship.

During the first decades of Roman rule there was extensive military action in Britain. The élite legionaries were trained to use their weapons in a highly lethal way. Shortly before giving battle to the British forces of Boudicca, the Roman general Paullinus reminded his legionaries of the ingredients of a successful military encounter:

> Keep close order, and once you have thrown your javelins, carry on cutting down and slaughtering the enemy with your shield bosses and swords, without any thought for booty.   *(Tacitus)*

Legionaries and auxiliaries worked together on major campaigns. This is clear from the literary sources and from archaeological evidence such as the excavations at Maiden Castle, Dorset, where there was a significant battle during the early stages of the Roman conquest. An analysis of the bones of the British casualties at Maiden Castle suggests that some of the defenders were killed by auxiliaries with long swords, while others received mortal blows from the distinctive short stabbing swords of the legionaries. The fighting at Maiden Castle was vicious. The dead included both men, women and children.

Senior officers were sometimes promoted from the ranks, others were aristocratic young noblemen spending time in the army as part of their careers. Campaigning in a place like Britain gave such young officers an opportunity to impress their superiors. One man who was part of the invasion force of AD 43 was Vespasian, the future emperor. His success in Britain greatly helped his later career. Vespasian undertook dangerous missions during

BELOW *A modern drawing of an armourer's hoard of scrap metal from Corbridge. It was buried in about AD 130*

ABOVE *A soldier's iron dagger from around AD 200, found in London*

ABOVE *Trajan's column in Rome gives a vivid picture of the many facets of military life. Here a camp is erected*

the early stages of the conquest. He and his brother went behind enemy lines. Later he appears to have campaigned with the Second Legion in the south and west of Britain. A biographer described how he conquered the Isle of Wight, fought thirty battles, defeated two tribes and captured twenty British settlements. He might well have commanded the Roman forces at the bloody battle of Maiden Castle.

While aristocratic officers built their reputations, life for auxiliaries was less glamorous. Auxiliaries were considered more expendable than legionaries and were often given some of the most dangerous missions. During the Roman invasion of AD 43, the British forces tried to use rivers to protect themselves from the Romans. The Roman commander responded by ordering Celtic auxiliaries to swim across these natural barriers:

> Plautius sent across some Celts who were practised at swimming with ease fully armed across even the fastest of rivers. These fell unexpectedly on the enemy, but rather than attacking the men they maimed the horses that drew the chariots instead. In the resulting confusion not even the mounted warriors could get away unscathed.
> *(Dio Cassius, early third century AD)*

The lower value placed on auxiliary lives is clear from the way the Roman general Agricola fought the British at a place called Mount Graupius in Scotland in about AD 83. He placed his auxiliary forces at the front and his legions at the rear, and the auxiliaries bore the brunt of the fighting. The historian Tacitus described these tactics approvingly and said that a victory involving auxiliary casualties but no legionary deaths would be 'glorious'

because it would 'cost no Roman blood'. These particular auxiliaries were Batavians from northern Gaul. They were well trained and well armed and they got the better of the disorganised British forces in vicious hand-to-hand fighting:

> The auxiliary infantry had been well drilled in sword-fighting, while the enemy were awkward at it. The Batavian auxiliaries, raining blow after blow, striking them with the bosses of their shields, and stabbing them in the face, felled the Britons on the plain… Equipment, bodies, and mangled limbs lay all around on the blood-stained earth.   *(Tacitus)*

Tacitus described the fight at Mount Graupius as a great triumph for Roman force. However, the Romans were not able to consolidate their control of northern Britain. In the following centuries the northern tribes seem to have preferred guerrilla warfare during the periods of conflict with Rome. Over a hundred years after the battle of Mount Graupius the Emperor Severus visited Britain and attempted to complete the work of Agricola by crushing the northern tribes. The guerrilla tactics of the British forces thwarted his plans.

> Wishing to subdue the whole of Britain, Severus invaded Caledonia, as he passed through it, he experienced untold difficulties in cutting down the forests, levelling the high ground, filling in the swamps, and bridging the rivers. He fought no battles nor did he see any enemy drawn up for battle. Instead they deliberately put sheep and cattle in the Romans' way for the soldiers to seize, so that they might be lured on further still and thus be worn out. In fact, the Romans suffered great hardships because of the water, and any stragglers became a prey to ambush. Then, unable to go on, they would be killed by their own men so they might not fall into enemy hands.
> *(Dio Cassius)*

ABOVE *Cavalrymen possessed equipment designed not for battle but for parade, such as this striking mask of iron with silver details*

LEFT *Soldiers needed to be occupied during their hours off duty. This board game, with its counters and dice, was found at Corbridge*

A POSTING TO BRITAIN

ABOVE *The tombstone of Longinus. He came from modern Bulgaria and died shortly after the Roman invasion*

For much of the first and second centuries AD the British garrison of the Roman army included three legions, made up of about 15,000 men and about 30,000 auxiliaries. In the early days of the Roman occupation the majority of these soldiers were from outside Britain. We know the origins of about seventy individual legionaries who took part in the invasion of Britain; eighty per cent were from Italy. After the middle of the first century AD, fewer men from Italy volunteered to join the legions. Of the known legionaries who were in Britain between AD 69 and 117, Italians were a small minority and after AD 117 hardly any legionaries came from Italy.

The first auxiliaries were also a cosmopolitan group of men. We know, for example, from a tombstone in Colchester of one Longinus Sdapeze, of the First Thracians, son of Matygus, from Sardica, in modern Bulgaria, who died aged forty after fifteen years of service. His unit was moved from Britain before AD 49, so he must have died or been killed at a very early stage in the occupation. He was a 'duplicarius', a cavalry trooper on double pay as a non-commissioned officer. In total there were about seventy known auxiliary regiments in Britain during the period of Roman rule: twenty were originally from Gaul, eighteen from the Danubian and Balkan lands, twelve from Germany and twelve from Spain. Integrating men from many lands and cultures into an effective fighting force was a remarkable achievement, and things did not always go well. Tacitus described how some Germanic auxiliaries in Britain turned on their Roman masters with unpleasant consequences:

That same summer a cohort of the Usipi that had been enrolled in Germany and transferred to Britain ventured upon a memorable exploit. They murdered a centurion and some soldiers who, to teach them discipline, were serving in their ranks as models and instructors. Then they boarded three small warships, forcing the pilots to do their will; but one of these escaped, and the other two were then looked upon with such suspicion that they were killed... The time came when they had to put into land to get water and other supplies. This brought them into collision with parties of Britons who tried to protect their property; and in the end they were so near starvation that they began to eat one another; first they picked out the weakest, then they drew lots. *(Tacitus)*

Emperors sometimes stationed auxiliary forces in Britain because they were not trustworthy and were best placed in a faraway, inaccessible place like Britain. In the 170s Marcus Aurelius struck a deal with enemy peoples in the Danube area. This involved the recruitment of enemy cavalry into the Roman army. Many of these mounted soldiers were transferred to Britain:

As their contribution to the alliance the Iazyges immediately provided Marcus Aurelius with 8,000 cavalry, 5,500 of whom he sent to Britain. *(Dio Cassius)*

A century later, in AD 277, Probus used a similar tactic when he sent barbarian prisoners of war to Britain for re-settlement:

He personally engaged the Burgundians and Vandals in battle. Those he was able to take alive he sent to Britain, where they settled and became useful to the Emperor when anyone later rebelled. *(Zosimus, fifth century AD)*

ABOVE *A knife or razor found at the Roman base at Vindolanda*

BELOW *A modern impression of legionaries on a route march. Military life could entail considerable hardships*

ABOVE *A mix of cultures: a stone carving of a Celtic head found within the Hadrian's Wall milecastle at Sewingshields*

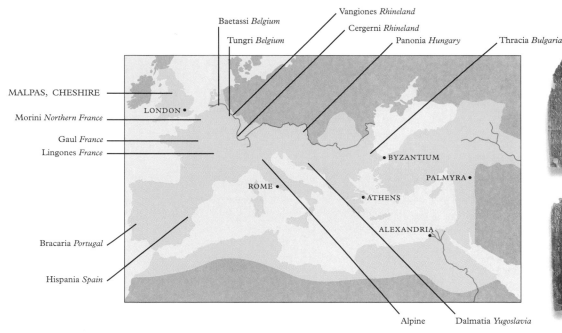

Baetassi *Belgium*
Tungri *Belgium*
Vangiones *Rhineland*
Cergerni *Rhineland*
Panonia *Hungary*
Thracia *Bulgaria*

MALPAS, CHESHIRE
Morini *Northern France*
Gaul *France*
Lingones *France*

LONDON

BYZANTIUM
PALMYRA
ROME
ATHENS
ALEXANDRIA

Bracaria *Portugal*

Hispania *Spain*

Alpine
Dalmatia *Yugoslavia*

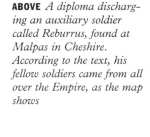

ABOVE *A diploma discharging an auxiliary soldier called Reburrus, found at Malpas in Cheshire. According to the text, his fellow soldiers came from all over the Empire, as the map shows*

It is impossible to know exactly how Roman soldiers felt about a posting to Britain. For many the climate was likely to be a shock. The letters that have been excavated at Vindolanda refer to the use of socks and underpants – items not normally found as part of Roman military uniform. Inscriptions on altars hint that some soldiers were homesick during their tour of Britain. At Maryport, Cornelius Peregrinus dedicated an altar to 'Fortune the Home Bringer'. Naevius Verus Roscianus was clearly relieved to get back from Britain; he erected an altar to celebrate his safe return in his home town of Piacenza.

Conversely, there is also evidence that some soldiers came to see Britain as their home. Many soldiers chose to spend their retirement in Britain. In Malpas, Cheshire, a bronze 'discharge diploma' has been discovered, belonging to Reburrus, an auxiliary cavalryman who had served with the First Pannonians. The diploma recorded how he retired and acquired Roman citizenship on 19 January AD 103, after twenty-five years service. (Citizenship gave one legal rights and privileges. Once an auxiliary was granted citizenship, all his children became citizens too.) Pannonia is in modern Hungary but the fact that the diploma was found in Cheshire indicates that he decided to spend his retirement in Britain. Officially, ordinary soldiers were not allowed to get married while in the army, but in reality many had permanent partners and children. Doubtless, many soldiers serving in Britain met British women and established families together.

After the early years of conquest and campaigning, there were probably long periods when there was no armed conflict and the emphasis was on training the troops to be prepared for war. The historian Josephus saw legionaries training and said that they took drill as seriously as war itself. Josephus considered this commitment to training to be the key to the success of the Romans under battle conditions. He commented that, 'it would not be far from the truth to call their drills "battles without blood" and their battles "blood-stained drills".' A much later military writer called Vegetius stressed the importance of drill as part of the basic training for new recruits:

The young soldiers must be given frequent practice in carrying loads of up to sixty pounds (about 28 kilograms), and marching along at military pace, for on strenuous campaigns they will be faced with the necessity of carrying their rations as well as their arms. Let this not be thought difficult, if practice is given; for there is nothing which constant practice does not make easy.
(Vegetius, fourth century AD)

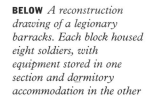

BELOW *A reconstruction drawing of a legionary barracks. Each block housed eight soldiers, with equipment stored in one section and dormitory accommodation in the other*

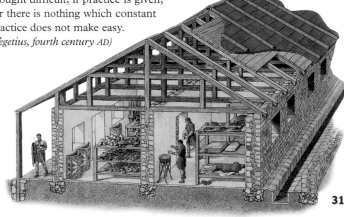

I WRITE THIS TO YOU FROM VINDOLANDA

To Paris of the third Cohort of Batavians from Sollemnis. Greetings. I want you to know that I am in very good health, as I hope you are in return, you neglectful man, who have sent me not even one letter. But I think I am behaving in a more considerate fashion in writing to you. Give my greetings to Diligens, Cogitatus and Corinthus.

This letter of reproach written by an officer in the Roman army to a friend was found at Vindolanda, a Roman fort in northern England. It is one of an enormous collection of documents that have come to light since the first letter was discovered in 1973. The Vindolanda documents are unique and they provide a vivid picture of life in Roman Britain. They were written on extremely thin 'tablets' or slices of wood, typically the size of a modern postcard. Unusual environmental conditions preserved the documents underground for nearly two thousand years. They date from about AD 100, a time when Vindolanda was the base for Batavians and Tungrians, auxiliary troops from northern Gaul.

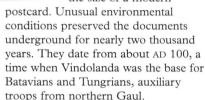

ABOVE *A letter from Vindolanda*

One of the Vindolanda texts is a strength report for a unit called the First Cohort of Tungrians. This is the only known example from Roman Britain of a detailed account of an army unit. The Tungrians at Vindolanda were led by a commander called Julius Verecundus. The text states that the total size of the unit was 752 men, but 456 soldiers, that is two-thirds of the total, were absent on duties elsewhere. Detachments from Vindolanda were serving at seven other locations, including a centurion working in London and a large force of 337 men posted to nearby Corbridge. One section of the writing is difficult to decipher but it seems to say that some of the soldiers had been posted to Gaul. The centurion in London was probably seconded to the staff of the provincial governor. Six men were listed as wounded; this is a small fraction of the total and it suggests that there was only limited armed conflict

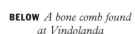

BELOW *A bone comb found at Vindolanda*

taking place at that time. A further twenty-five men were ill, including ten suffering from 'inflammation of the eyes'. As a result of absence and illness, Julius Verecundus was only able to call on 265 soldiers fit for active service at Vindolanda. The letters contain very few references to the enemy. In one brief text there is an evaluation of the fighting strength of the British. It describes how they fight without armour and swords and use cavalry, referring to them dismissively as 'Brittunculi', meaning 'the wretched Britons'.

Many of the Vindolanda documents were written by Batavian officers and their families. They originated from the area around the mouth of the Rhine/Scheldt. Unlike most auxiliary forces, the Batavians were allowed to have senior officers drawn from their own people. The commander, or 'prefect', of the Batavians at Vindolanda was one Flavius Cerialis. His Latin name celebrated the fact that he was a successful Roman citizen. He was a wealthy man because only those with substantial landed property were allowed to command army units. Cerialis features prominently in the Vindolanda documents, and he was obviously a powerful man. His correspondents are often deferential and address him as 'my lord'; one officer described him as 'his king'. He had considerable patronage at his disposal and was often asked for favours. In several letters, soldiers ask Cerialis permission to go on leave; in one he is asked to look favourably on someone looking for a post as an officer. Officers of detachments who were stationed outside the fort wrote to Cerialis to ask for instructions and to make requests. Some of these requests were surprising:

Please, my lord, give instructions as to what you want to have done tomorrow. My fellow-soldiers have no beer. Please order some to be sent.

While those at Vindolanda looked to Cerialis for help and advancement, he, in turn, sought favours from officials close to the provincial governor in London. In one letter Cerialis tried to ingratiate himself with a high official named Crispinus:

ABOVE *The Corbridge Lion. This was part of a fountain at Corbridge. Many of the men of Vindolanda were seconded to serve at nearby Corbridge*

BELOW *An iron knife with a carved bone handle from Vindolanda*

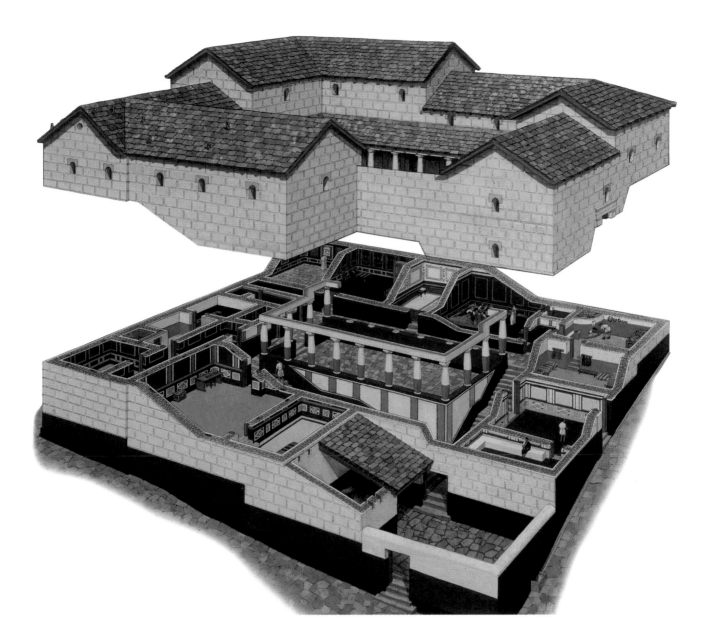

To his Crispinus. I have gladly seized the opportunity, my lord, of greeting you, you who are my lord and the man whom it is my very special wish to be in good health and master of all your hopes… Furnish me with very many friends that thanks to you I may be able to enjoy a pleasant period of military service. I write this to you from Vindolanda where my winter-quarters are.

Cerialis and his fellow officers lived well, despite their great distance from the heart of the Roman Empire. In one letter a writer mentions appreciatively that he has been sent fifty oysters. Another officer writes to a slave and tells him to obtain '100 apples, if you can find nice ones and 100 or 200 eggs, if they are for sale there at a fair price'. Another document itemises the food consumed by officers over a number of days one June. The most frequent items are locally-produced barley and Celtic beer. Other entries include imported fish-sauce and wine. One of the popular wines was Massic, an expensive drink from Italy. Another account described the great variety of meats consumed by the officers of Vindolanda: chicken, goat-meat, pork, ham and venison. They had particular tastes, and enjoyed such delicacies as pigs' trotters and pork crackling, but there are no references to lamb or mutton although we know from archaeological evidence that sheep were plentiful at the time.

ABOVE *The lavish quarters of the commanding officer at Vindolanda in the second century AD. Men like Cerialis enjoyed a very high status and this was reflected in their accommodation*

RULING BRITANNIA

For the first two centuries of Roman rule Britain was a single province of the Empire and the provincial governor controlled both the army of Britain and much of the civil administration. We know quite a lot about the early governors of the province of Britannia. They came from the senatorial class, the highest rank of imperial society. The governors were wealthy aristocrats and they had usually already held very senior posts in the imperial administration before their posting to Britain. Governors typically spent between three and four years on their tour of duty in Britain, before moving on to a further post or retiring. At least one governor went on to become emperor.

The British governorship was regarded as an important prize by ambitious senatorial Romans. It seems that only Syria was more highly regarded. Why did these men view a posting to the distant province of Britain so favourably? The answer seems to lie in the unusual concentration of military power in Britain. The governor had responsibility for the army and the defence of the province. He appointed his own senior officers and the large size of the British garrison gave each governor considerable powers of patronage.

The governor was the chief dispenser of justice. Although based in London, he also travelled around the province in order to make judgements in serious legal cases. Ulpianus, an influential Roman legal writer, stressed the key part that the governor should play in making the Roman system of justice work:

> It is proper for a good and conscientious governor to take care that the province which he governs is peaceful and quiet. He will accomplish this without difficulty if he works carefully to hunt down bad men and free the province of them; for he must hunt down sacrilegious persons, robbers, kidnappers and thieves, and punish each according to his crime.
> *(Ulpianus, third century AD)*

While the governorship of Britain was a prestigious post, it was also a challenging one. Maintaining control of a newly conquered territory was often difficult. Tacitus criticised one governor, Vettius Bolanus, for being insufficiently ruthless, saying, 'Britain at that time was governed with a hand too gentle for a warlike province.' The world of high imperial politics was not without risk. According to the historian Suetonius, the Emperor Domitian executed the governor of Britain in a fit of pique and jealousy:

> Domitian put to death many senators including a number of ex-consuls. Among them was Sallustius Lucullus, Governor of Britain, because he allowed a new type of spear to be called Lucullan. *(Suetonius)*

Although governors were members of the most privileged class in Roman society, there was some social mobility and the senatorial class was not a closed caste. The career of one governor called Pertinax powerfully illustrates this fact. He was the son of a former slave and he was a school teacher until the age of thirty-four. He changed direction and joined the army, and meteoric promotion ultimately led to membership of the senate, the governorship of Britain and, finally, the imperial crown itself in AD 193. His governorship of Britain was not a very happy experience, though:

> Pertinax put down revolts against himself in Britain and indeed came into very great danger, being almost killed in a mutiny involving a legion and left among the dead. This Pertinax punished with signal severity, but eventually he asked to be relieved of his post as governor, saying that the legions were hostile to him on account of his maintenance of discipline. *(Scriptores Historiae Augustae)*

Governors had great power but the imperial system ensured that each governor had a local rival. To stop corruption, the Emperor Augustus insisted that taxation and other money

ABOVE *This tombstone fragment shows a Roman military administrator, with a pack of writing tablets. The governor of the province controlled a considerable administrative and military machine*

ABOVE *An inkpot and pen, from the first century AD*

CENTRE *Governors often went on military campaigns. This coin of the second century AD shows Britannia and celebrates a victory in the province*

ABOVE *The governor was based in London. The civic life of the capital centred on the enormous basilica building, depicted above in this reconstruction drawing*

matters should be handled, not by the governor, but by another high official known as the procurator. The massive tombstone of one first-century procurator called Classicianus was discovered in London, where he died while in post. There was, inevitably, often tension between governor and procurator. We know that Classicianus fell out with the governor, Paullinus, and complained to Rome about his behaviour. Tacitus described their difficult relationship:

Two were now set over them – a governor to vent his fury on their life-blood, a Procurator on their property. Whether these overlords worked as a team or were at each other's throat was equally ruinous for those under them. The agents of either, centurions on one side, slaves on the other, added insult to injury… Julius Classicianus was on bad terms with Suetonius Paullinus and allowed his personal

animosity to stand in the way of the national interest. He was giving out that it would be well to await a new governor. He reported to Rome that they should expect no end to hostilities unless a replacement was found for Suetonius, whose failures he attributed to the man's incompetence, his successes to chance. *(Tacitus)*

LEFT *The British Museum contains the splendid tomb of Classicianus, a procurator who died while serving in Britain*

WOMEN OF THE EMPIRE

ABOVE *A wall-painting from Pompeii showing a woman with a pen and a book. Correspondence between Roman army wives has been excavated at Vindolanda*

BELOW *An inscribed copper alloy disc from London showing a young girl. Archaeologists think that this might have been used as a token in a brothel*

LEFT *A carved relief showing a man much larger than his wife. In law, women were subordinate to men*

was reflected in the way in which women derived their names. Roman women in Britain who followed traditional practice had two names: the family name and a female version of their father's name. Thus a tombstone from Chesters commemorates a girl called Fabia Honorata, who was the daughter of an army officer called Fabius Honoratus.

In Roman law a woman could marry at the age of twelve. Tombstone evidence from Britain suggests that most women might have married significantly later. The youngest known married woman living in Roman Britain was called Claudia Martina. She was the wife of a senior imperial administrator and she died in London aged nineteen. In law, divorce was very easy, and it was often enough for a man to say, 'wife, get out of the house', and the marriage was dissolved.

Letters found at Vindolanda shed light on the domestic lives of army wives. We know that a woman called Sulpicia Lepidina was the wife of the fort commander, Flavius Cerialis, in about AD 100. There are archaeological traces of family life at the fort. Children's shoes, for example, have been found in the area of the commander's residence. Archaeologists have also found a tablet that may well be a writing exercise carried out by one of

Senior Roman officers and administrators on postings to Britain were often accompanied by their wives. Some traditionalists disapproved of this; Tacitus quoted Caecina Severus, a man who argued that officers' wives caused trouble:

> An entourage of women involves luxury in peacetime and panic in wartime. It turns the Roman army into the likeness of a procession of barbarians. Not only is the female sex weak and unable to bear hardship but, when it has the freedom, it is spiteful, ambitious and greedy for power. They disport themselves among the soldiers and have the centurions eating out of their hands. *(Tacitus)*

Roman law denied women independence. Every woman was under the authority of a male 'guardian', typically her father or husband. Cicero justified this by reference to the intelligence of women: 'Our ancestors established the rule that all women, because of their weakness of intellect, should be under the power of guardians.' Male dominance

ABOVE *A jet necklace from Dorchester*

Sulpicia's children. The text includes a line from Virgil's *Aeneid*, a poem that was often used for school exercises. Lepidina corresponded with other officers' wives. One intriguing letter is an invitation for Lepidina to attend a friend's birthday party:

> ◆ Claudia Severa to her Lepidina, greetings. On the third day before the Ides of September, sister, for the celebration of my birthday, I give you a warm invitation to make sure that you come to us, to make the day more enjoyable for me by your arrival… Give my greeting to your Cerialis. My Aelius and my little son send… their greetings. I shall expect you, sister. Farewell, sister, my dearest soul.

The sender of the birthday party invitation was Claudia Severa, the wife of another officer called Aelius Brocchus. Life as an officer's wife in a strange land must have been difficult and Lepidina and Severa seem to have provided mutual support. Their stay in Britain was not a permanent one. An inscription from Hungary indicates that Brocchus and Severa were later posted to the Danube area, where Brocchus commanded a cavalry unit.

The mobility of Severa was typical of the early days of the Roman Empire and there are several other examples of army wives having to endure moves across huge distances. We know, for example, of one Claudia Marcia Capitolina, who lived in York where one of her sons was born, before moving all the way to Arabia. For many of these women the posting to the cold northern frontier of the Empire must have been a considerable shock. One woman, called Julia Lucilla, who came from a distinguished Roman senatorial family, found herself living at High Rochester, an outpost fort in dangerous territory beyond Hadrian's Wall. Her husband, Rufinus, had previously held prestigious posts in the city of Rome itself. Julia Lucilla must have found life in an isolated fort in northern Britain very different to her old life in the great city of Rome.

Other distinguished women also visited Britain. Between AD 208 and 211 the Empress Julia Domna accompanied her husband Severus during his stay in Britain. She was renowned for her intelligence and learning, and while she was in Britain she also showed that she had a vivacious personality. Dio Cassius relates how, at the time of the signing of a treaty, Julia Domna chatted jokingly with the wife of a Caledonian chief. The empress criticised the Caledonian women because, she said, they had lots of lovers. The Caledonian woman was not prepared to be lectured by the empress and she replied, 'We fulfil nature's demands much better than you Roman women do: we openly associate with the best men, you commit adultery with the worst in private.'

While officers were allowed to bring their wives to Britain, the situation for ordinary soldiers was very different. Officially soldiers below the rank of centurion were not allowed to marry before an edict of AD 197. There is little doubt, however, that many soldiers did have female partners and that they often followed their menfolk to Britain, as unofficial 'wives' are mentioned in many of the surviving discharge documents. When units became established in permanent forts, settlements grew up ouside their gates. Archaeologists think that these settlement or 'vici' often housed the women of the ordinary soldiers.

The wives of senior officers lived in some comfort. The commandant's house at Housesteads has been extensively excavated. It was a handsome courtyard house built in the style of a substantial Roman townhouse. It was the largest single building in the fort and reflected the very high status of the fort's commandant and his family. The house was frequently altered as different commandants came and went; the standard tour of duty was three years and many wives might have disliked the taste of their predecessors. The dining-room and other grand rooms were provided with underfloor heating. There was a lavatory, a bath suite and a large kitchen. Traces of wall plaster have been discovered, suggesting that the walls might once have been decorated. The house also incorporated stables, probably with servants' quarters above.

BRITAIN AND THE EMPIRE

Although Britain was on the edge of the Empire, it was seen as a prize worth winning, and successive emperors tried to conquer it. Some tribal chieftains made peace with the Romans, but others actively resisted, including Caratacus and Boudicca. The Romans were never able to pacify the whole of the island.

CAESAR IN BRITAIN

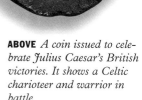

ABOVE *A coin issued to celebrate Julius Caesar's British victories. It shows a Celtic charioteer and warrior in battle*

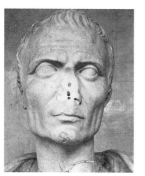

ABOVE *A marble bust of Julius Caesar*

The power of Rome had a dramatic impact on British history during the years 55 and 54 BC as Roman forces, led by the great commander Julius Caesar, invaded Britain. The expedition of 55 BC took place late in the summer, shortly before the end of the usual campaigning season. Caesar took with him a relatively small force of two legions and some auxiliary units. The size of the force and the lateness of the season suggests that Caesar saw the expedition as a preliminary reconnaissance mission. We have a highly informative but deeply biased source for the expeditions of Caesar, in his own book of memoirs, *The Gallic Wars*. In these memoirs Caesar gave a brief portrait of Britain and its people. Modern scholars think that we should view Caesar's judgements with great caution but they still make for interesting reading:

> The population is very large, their homesteads thick on the ground and very much like those in Gaul, and the cattle numerous… All the Britons dye themselves with woad, and as a result their appearance in battle is all the more daunting. They wear their hair long, and shave all their bodies with the exception of their heads and upper lips. Wives are shared between groups of ten or twelve men, especially between brothers and between fathers and sons. *(Julius Caesar)*

In Caesar's account, the expeditions to Britain are relatively brief episodes within his narrative of how he personally conquered Gaul on behalf of the Roman republic. Caesar justified the attack on Britain on the grounds that the Britons had provided military help to the people of Gaul. Modern historians are sceptical about whether this explanation provides the full story. An alternative theory is that Caesar knew that his enemies in Rome were plotting against him. Campaigning in Britain was useful because it gave him prestige back in Rome, and while he was a commander on active service he enjoyed immunity from prosecution.

Before his departure for Britain, Caesar held a conference with merchants who traded with Britain, to discover what he could about the lie of the land. Despite this precaution the expedition of 55 BC went wrong almost immediately. The ships transporting the cavalry were delayed and failed to meet up with the infantry forces. The British had got word of Caesar's plans and a large armed force greeted the Romans on their arrival. Caesar found it difficult to find a suitable landing place, and the legionaries, with their heavy armour and equipment, were forced to make their way through deep sea water, while the Britons attacked them on the beach. These scenes were graphically recalled by Caesar:

> Our soldiers, in a foreign land, with their hands full, burdened with heavy armour, had to leap from the ships and standing in the middle of the waves, encounter the enemy. Dismayed by these circumstances and completely unused to this kind of fighting, our men did not show their usual vigour and eagerness.

The panicking troops were somewhat rallied by the eagle-bearer of the Tenth Legion who shouted:

> Jump down, comrades, unless you wish to betray your eagle to the enemy; it shall be told that I at any rate did my duty to the republic and my general.

Fierce and difficult fighting followed on the beach before the Romans eventually secured their bridgehead. Without cavalry Caesar was restricted in his ability to advance much further. His fleet of transport ships was then damaged by a storm. This constituted

BELOW *The shield of a British nobleman at about the time of Julius Caesar's expeditions. It was found in the River Witham*

a major crisis for the Romans who were not equipped to spend the winter in Britain. Sensing the degree of Roman weakness, the British forces gathered for the kill. Caesar described in his memoirs how his own masterly leadership saved the day for the beleaguered Romans and how the legions safely returned to Gaul for the winter.

In 54 BC Caesar once more set sail for Britain, with a much more substantial force of five legions and 2000 cavalry. Over the winter he had also assembled an enormous fleet of more than 800 ships. The Britons were alarmed at this powerful invading force and no resistance was offered as they landed. Before the Romans could really impose their authority on their British enemy, the Roman fleet at anchor was damaged by a storm. Caesar described how hasty action was required to create a strongly fortified camp and to repair the ships. The fighting between the Britons and the Romans was inconclusive: after some preliminary skirmishes it seems that the Britons decided to avoid a pitched battle. The Romans responded by ravaging the land as they marched through part of south-east Britain. Caesar described how the British eventually sued for peace and promised to pay tribute. As the summer was almost over Caesar then returned his forces to Gaul.

It is not clear whether Caesar intended to return the following year to secure a conquest. Whatever his plans, he was overtaken by events. Shortly after returning from Britain he learnt that his beloved only daughter, Julia, had died in childbirth. A major rebellion then broke out in Gaul. Caesar had no opportunity to revisit Britain, as he struggled to maintain Roman authority on the other side of

the Channel. As a result Britain remained free of Roman control for the best part of a century following the expeditions of 55 and 54 BC.

Caesar's account of his visits to Britain is an exercise in self-publicity. Some other Roman writers took a different, and rather jaundiced view of his trips to Britain. We get a fascinating alternative slant on the invasions of Britain from the letters of Cicero, who had contacts with the invading force. His brother Quintus and friend Trebatius both accompanied Caesar and corresponded with Cicero. He wrote, for example, to Trebatius in June 54 BC in a way that suggests that he was unimpressed by the news from Britain: 'I hear there's no gold and silver in Britain. If this is so, I advise you to get a war-chariot and hasten back to us as soon as possible.' Shortly before the end of the campaign Cicero wrote to his brother indicating that the adventure in Britain did not amount to very much: 'On affairs in Britain I see from your letter there is nothing to fear or rejoice at.' Writing over a century later the historian Tacitus also sought to minimise Caesar's achievement:

◆ Julius Caesar, the first Roman to enter Britain with an army, did indeed intimidate the natives by a victory and secure a grip on the coast. But he may fairly be said to have merely drawn attention to the island. *(Tacitus)*

BELOW *A Roman military vessel with soldiers about to leap ashore. During Julius Caesar's first expedition, the legionaries were attacked as they attempted to disembark*

ABOVE *A coin of Julius Caesar bearing his famous words 'I came, I saw, I conquered'. Some other leading Romans were less impressed by Caesar's British adventures*

TOP *The memory of Julius Caesar lived on long after his death. This is a copy of a Renaissance painting by Mantegna illustrating Caesar in triumph*

39

CLAUDIUS AND THE CONQUEST OF BRITAIN

ABOVE *A drawing of a relief showing Britannia lying prostrate before the power of Rome*

legions and a large force of auxiliaries, led by Aulus Plautius, to attack Britain. Plautius was an experienced general, with a successful track record but the invasion did not get off to a good start. As in the days of Caligula, the troops had no wish to embark on a hazardous trip across the Channel to a place that they saw as the edge of the world. They threatened mutiny when ordered to Britain:

> Plautius had difficulty getting his army to leave Gaul, since the troops were indignant at the prospect of campaigning outside the known world and would not obey him.   *(Dio Cassius)*

In the year AD 41 the Emperor Caligula was assassinated and his uncle Claudius found himself on the imperial throne. A year earlier Caligula had led a bizarre attempt to invade Britain. He had assembled a military force and naval vessels at Boulogne for the crossing to Britain only to discover that the legionaries had no wish to go on this hazardous adventure. He responded by putting briefly out to sea and claiming that he had conquered the ocean by this act, and then ordering his legionaries to gather sea-shells as trophies of his victory. These shells were taken back to Rome to be displayed proudly as the booty of war.

After the death of Caligula, the new emperor was in a weak position and needed a military victory to consolidate his power. Claudius chose Britain as the scene of his anticipated triumph, and two years after his accession he launched an attack on the island. Claudius was fascinated by his imperial predecessors and full of admiration for Julius Caesar. Through the conquest of Britain he hoped to outdo the great Caesar, who had failed to secure Roman control of the island.

In AD 43 Claudius ordered four

A senior imperial official called Narcissus tried to speak to the legionaries in order to persuade them to obey the command to go to Britain. At first this made matters worse, as Narcissus was a former slave and the legionaries were incensed at the idea of an ex-slave telling them what to do. The mood changed when some began to chant, as a joke, the traditional cry of 'Io Saturnalia!' used on the feast of Saturnalia, the one day of the year when slaves were allowed to give orders to their masters. The cry was taken up by all and the fickle legionaries then agreed to embark for Britain.

In the decades before the Roman invasion the dominant figure in southeast Britain was the Catuvellaunian chieftain, Cunobelinus – later immortalised by Shakespeare as Cymbeline. One of his strongholds was at Colchester, known to the Romans as Camulodunum. Cunobelinus died shortly before the coming of the Romans and his lands were divided

ABOVE *A reconstruction drawing showing daily life on the eve of the invasion*

ABOVE *The Emperor Claudius. He looked to Britain for a military triumph*

CENTRE *A coin with an elephant. The inhabitants of Colchester must have been amazed when they saw Claudius and his war-elephants*

between two of his sons. One of these sons, Caratacus, was to be the main leader of British resistance against the early stages of the Roman take-over.

The Romans marched through Kent and after some preliminary skirmishes defeated a British force at a major battle, probably at the River Medway. The Britons fled across the Thames and the Romans encountered some problems as they tried to follow them. Our sources stress the vital help that Celtic auxiliaries – probably from northern Gaul – gave to the legionaries:

> The Britons withdrew to the Thames, at a point where it flows into the sea. This they crossed with ease since they knew precisely where the ground was firm and the way passable. The Romans, however, in pursuing them got into difficulties here. Once again the Celtic auxiliaries swam across, while others crossed by a bridge a little way upstream, and they engaged the enemy from several sides at once, cutting many of them down. However, in pursuing the survivors without due precaution they got into the marshes from which it was difficult to find a way out and lost a number of men.

Having crossed the Thames, the way was clear for an attack on the stronghold of Colchester, which was seen as the enemy capital. At this point Plautius stopped and waited for the arrival of Claudius from Rome. To overawe the enemy, Claudius brought with him a number of war-elephants. Doubtless the people of Colchester were suitably impressed by the extraordinary sight of the emperor of Rome, with his elephants and his entourage, triumphantly marching into their settlement. Scholars disagree about whether Claudius was involved in any serious fighting, or whether he timed his crossing of the Channel so that he could enter Colchester in glory once the Britons no longer posed a serious threat:

> After sailing down river to Ostia he was then conveyed along the coast to Massilia. From there he travelled partly overland and partly along the rivers. On his arrival at Ocean [the Channel] he crossed over to Britain and joined the army, which was waiting for him at the Thames. Taking over command, he crossed the river and engaging the natives who had

gathered at his approach, defeated them, and took Camulodunum, the capital of Cunobelinus. Claudius returned to Rome after an absence of six months, of which he had spent only sixteen days in Britain.
> *(Dio Cassius)*

Claudius was immensely proud of his feats in Britain, and coins were struck in celebration. He ordered a programme of extensive festivities in the city of Rome: horse races, bear-baiting, athletics competitons and a celebratory war-dance by 'boys brought from Asia'. He renamed his young son, Britannicus. A triumphal arch was eventually erected in Rome to commemorate the victory. The inscription on the arch itemised his achievements in Britain in a way that implied that he had outdone his predecessors including, of course, Julius Caesar:

> He received the surrender of eleven British kings, defeated without any reverse, and was the first to bring barbarian tribes beyond Ocean under Roman sway.

In reality, the campaign of AD 43 only gave the Romans control of the south-eastern corner of the island. Writing half a century later, the biographer Suetonius put Claudius and his British adventure in perspective. He described how Claudius decided to attack Britain simply because it was the place where a military victory 'could be most readily obtained'. The British expedition was the only military campaign undertaken by Claudius and the overall judgement of Suetonius was that this 'sole campaign was of no great importance'.

BELOW *The Roman fort at Richborough. This was probably the place of entry for the invasion force of AD 43*

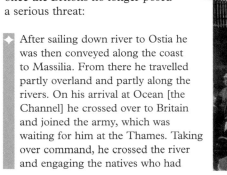

REBELLION!

The response of the British élite to the arrival of the Romans was very mixed. Some tribal chieftains made peace with the invaders and became rulers of 'client states' on behalf of Rome, while others continued to resist the Roman presence with force. There were rewards for those who collaborated. Cogidumnus, who ruled over the people of the Sussex and Hampshire area, was made a Roman citizen and was probably the owner of the magnificent Roman-style palace at Fishbourne. The Romans symbolically established a legionary fortress and later a Roman-style city at Colchester, formerly the stronghold of the British leader, Cunobelinus. Meanwhile his son Caratacus remained free and organised anti-Roman forces from bases in Wales. Eventually, in AD 51, Caratacus was defeated by a Roman army and he fled north to the court of the Brigantian ruler, a woman called Cartimandua. Unfortunately for Caratacus, Cartimandua was a collaborator and she handed him over to the Romans. Caratacus and his family were taken to Rome, where they were displayed in chains, as trophies of war. Tacitus described how Caratacus was paraded before the Roman public:

◆ The fame of Caratacus had reached beyond the islands and had spread through the adjoining provinces; in Italy too it was on people's lips, and folks longed to see who it was had defied our power for so many years. Even in Rome the name of Caratacus was well known. The people were summoned as if to a great spectacle; the Praetorian Cohorts were drawn up under arms on the parade ground in front of their camp. Then as the king's vassals filed past, the ornamental bosses, torques, and spoils won in his foreign wars were paraded. Next his brothers, wife, and daughter were displayed, and finally Caratacus himself. The others out of fear indulged in undignified pleading, but from Caratacus there was no downcast look, no appeal for mercy. *(Tacitus)*

ABOVE *This pot containing 872 Iceni coins was found in 1982. It was probably hidden during the rebellion of Boudicca*

Caratacus probably expected that he and his family would be put to death after their public humiliation. According to Tacitus he made a dignified speech in which he described his own distinguished ancestry, lamented his plight and asked for mercy. Claudius was moved by this and ordered that Caratacus and his family should be pardoned and released from their chains.

The defeat of Caratacus provided the Romans with an opportunity to consolidate their control of Britain. However, the Romans disastrously failed to win over all of the leaders of British society. The result was a rebellion so violent that it shook the foundations of Roman rule in Britain. The rebellion began among the Iceni people of the Norfolk area, who had been ruled over by a king called Prasutagus. He died in AD 60 and bequeathed his kingdom jointly to his daughters and the Roman emperor. By this act he indicated that the Iceni were

ABOVE *A nineteenth-century painting of captive Britons in Rome, by Thomas Davidson*

prepared to collaborate with Rome but the Roman authorities responded in a heavy-handed way, seizing the lands of the Iceni and treating the Iceni nobility as if they had been defeated in battle. Boudicca, the widow of Prasutagus, was flogged and her two daughters raped. This act was the spark that lit the fire of rebellion. Boudicca was clearly a remarkable woman and she responded to her mistreatment by leading the warriors of the Iceni, and the neighbouring tribe of the Trinovantes, in a great uprising. Dio Cassius provided a vivid description of the personal appearance of the British leader:

◆ In stature she was very tall and grim in appearance, with a piercing gaze and a harsh voice. She had a mass of very fair hair which she grew down to her hips, and wore a great gold torque and a multicoloured tunic folded round her, over which was a thick cloak fastened with a brooch. This was how she always dressed.
(Dio Cassius)

The early stages of the rebellion were helped by the fact that the Roman provincial governor, Paullinus, was far away, campaigning in Anglesey. In the absence of Paullinus, the most senior Roman official was the procurator, Decianus Catus. He failed to take decisive action and eventually fled to safety in Gaul. The first target of the rebels was the Roman settlement at Colchester, where retired legionaries were living on the site of the former British stronghold:

◆ Their bitterest hatred was directed against the veteran soldiers recently settled at the colony of Camulodunum, who were driving the natives from their homes, forcing them off their land, and calling them prisoners and slaves. The temple dedicated to the deified Claudius was looked upon as a stronghold of eternal tyranny. Nor did it seem difficult to destroy a colony that was unprotected by any fortifications, something to which our commander, putting comfort before necessity, had paid too little attention.

The small garrison at Colchester positioned itself in and around the massive temple to Claudius. After a siege of two days Boudicca took the temple and massacred the Romans. Shortly afterwards she intercepted part of the Ninth Legion and slaughtered the legionaries, and only the cavalry

managed to escape. The governor, Paullinus, raced back from Anglesey and assessed the situation in London. He decided that the position was desperate and that he could not defend London. He abandoned the city and allowed the forces of Boudicca to take and destroy both London and Verulamium (modern St Albans). The decision to pull out of London was a death sentence for those left behind:

◆ Neither the tears nor lamentations of those who begged his help could deflect Paullinus from giving the signal to pull out and allowing into his column only those who could keep up with him. Those who stayed behind because their sex meant they were unfit for war, or who were burdened with age or were attached to the place, were overwhelmed by the enemy. The same disaster befell St Albans. It is reckoned that 70,000 citizens and provincials fell in the places I have mentioned; for the enemy did not take or sell prisoners, nor was there any other traffic of war. Instead they rushed to slaughter, hang, burn and crucify.
(Tacitus)

Paullinus reorganised his forces in the Midlands and, when he felt ready, eventually confronted Boudicca in a pitched battle. His forces were outnumbered by the Britons but they benefited from a superior position on a hill-side and from better discipline. The army of Boudicca was destroyed with great loss of life. The queen herself escaped but died shortly afterwards and the great rebellion was over.

AGRICOLA: GOVERNOR OF ROMAN BRITAIN

Much of our knowledge of life during the Roman period comes from the great wealth of surviving archaeological evidence. There are also a few key documents that have been preserved from Roman times. One of the most informative of these rare documents is a biography of Agricola, who was the governor of Britain between AD 78 and 84. Written by his admiring son-in-law, Tacitus, the biography gives a fascinating, if one-sided, picture of Britain during the early days of Roman rule.

Agricola's career was typical of a leading member of the Roman aristocracy in that he held several important posts in the army and the imperial administration. More unusually his career took him to Britain on several different occasions. At the age of about twenty-one he was in

BELOW *A Roman school scene. Agricola consciously used education as a way of assimilating wealthy Britons into Roman ways of thinking*

ABOVE *A reconstruction drawing of the forum at Wroxeter. Agricola hoped that Roman civic amenities would convince Britons of the benefits of Roman rule*

RIGHT *A carving from Scotland showing a Roman cavalryman trampling down his enemy. Agricola campaigned in the north in his attempt to secure Roman control over the whole of Britain*

Britain as a senior military officer shortly after the rebellion of Boudicca. Ten years later he returned to Britain to take charge of the Twentieth Legion. Agricola also served in Asia, Gaul and the city of Rome before his third and final tour of duty in Britain as governor.

When Agricola arrived as governor, Britain was far from peaceful. His first objective was the destruction of the warlike Ordovices tribe of Wales. Agricola immediately marched to the Welsh mountains, where his men 'cut to pieces almost the whole fighting force of the tribe'. Agricola then proceeded to conquer Anglesey, which had long been seen as a centre of anti-Roman resistance. He had no fleet to help him and his troops surprised the inhabitants of Anglesey by audaciously swimming across the Menai Straits.

In Britain, as elsewhere in the Empire, the Romans sought to control their subjects by the use of both 'carrot and stick'. We see this in the way that Agricola, in addition to his energetic military campaigning, sought to improve life for British people. He encouraged the building of good new houses, together with impressive public squares and temples. Agricola shrewdly offered a Roman education to the sons of the British nobility. 'Instead of loathing the Latin language they became eager to speak it effectively. In the same way, our national dress came into favour and the toga was everywhere to be seen.'

Having pacified Wales, Agricola devoted much of his time as governor to the conquest of northern Britain. His forces took control of Scotland, south of the key rivers Clyde and Forth and then pushed further north. His intention was the complete conquest of the island of Britain. A legionary fortress was established at Inchtuthil, near the River Tay. The campaign in Scotland involved many problems for Agricola. The Caledonian tribes launched a surprise attack on the camp of the Ninth Legion and came close to defeating them before Agricola was able to arrive with reinforcements.

Agricola's career in Britain came to a climax when his forces confronted the tribes of northern Scotland at the Battle of Mount Graupius. The exact location of this battle is not known, although it was somewhere in north-east Scotland. Tacitus calculated that the British army was 30,000

BELOW This bronze helmet was probably worn by an auxiliary soldier at about the time of Agricola

strong and was led by a Caledonian called Calgacus. Tacitus gives an account of the speech that Calgacus made before the fighting began. The speech cannot be an accurate transcript but it gives us insights into attitudes at the time:

> ◆ We, the most distant dwellers upon earth, the last of the free, have been shielded till today by our very remoteness. Now, the farthest bounds of Britain lie open to our enemies. There are no more nations beyond us; nothing is there but waves and rocks.

Calgacus criticised the Romans for their aggression. In a memorable phrase he said of the Romans 'they create desolation and call it peace'. Tacitus also gives us the speech made by Agricola to the Roman forces:

ABOVE Three legionary soldiers. Despite the victory at Mount Graupius the legions were not able to complete the conquest of Britain

> ◆ The farthest boundary of this land, we hold in our grasp. Many a time on the march, as you trudged wearily over marshes, mountains and rivers, have I heard the bravest among you exclaim: 'When shall we meet the enemy? When will they come and fight us?' They are coming now, for we have dug them out of their hiding-places.

The Romans defeated the British army at the Battle of Mount Graupius. When news of this great victory reached Rome, the Emperor Domitian was curiously unhappy. He was said to be jealous of the military success of Agricola, and he recalled Agricola to Rome. The great man lived on for another decade in quiet retirement.

HADRIAN AND THE LIMITS OF ROMAN RULE

The Emperor Hadrian came to power in AD 117. Unlike earlier emperors, he made no attempt to win glory by new conquests. On the contrary, he abandoned some of the territories in the east conquered by his predecessor, Trajan. Instead of increasing the size of the Empire, Hadrian put his considerable energies into securing its defences. The building of Hadrian's Wall was, therefore, part of a grand Empire-wide policy of retrenchment and consolidation. Hadrian restlessly toured the Empire, inspecting and seeking to improve the capacity and readiness of the army. It seems that not all his entourage enjoyed his peripatetic lifestyle. A court poet called Florus wrote a good-natured criticism of

BELOW *A bronze bust of the Emperor Hadrian. He restlessly toured the Empire seeking to strengthen its defences*

Hadrian's journeys and the discomforts associated with constant travel:

> I don't want to be emperor, please,
> To tramp round Britain, weak at
>   the knees,
> Or in the Scythian winter to freeze.
> *(Florus, second century AD)*

Florus refers to Hadrian's visits to places as far apart as Scythia (in the modern Ukraine) and Britain. The British visit took place in AD 122 and it was probably at this time that the momentous decision was taken to build a wall across the entire island, from the Solway Firth in the west to the lower reaches of the Tyne in the east. A much later fourth-century document gives a brief account of Hadrian's visit to Britain and the building of the wall:

BELOW *A reconstruction drawing of Wallsend Fort. This fort guarded the eastern end of the wall*

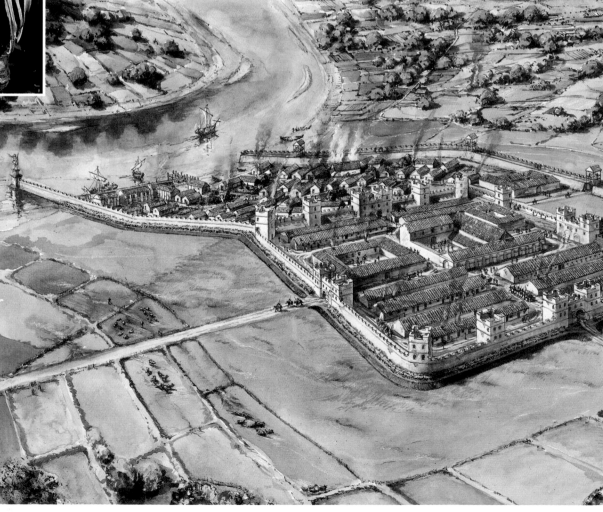

ABOVE *The Rudge cup is an unusual Roman souvenir of the wall. It shows the wall and some of its forts*

Hadrian devoted his energies to maintaining peace throughout the world… Having reformed the army in the manner of a king, Hadrian set out for Britain. There he corrected many faults and was the first to build a wall eighty miles long, to separate the Romans and the barbarians.
(Scriptores Historia Augustae)

While little is known of Hadrian's stay in Britain, it is safe to assume that, as in other provinces, he spent much of his time inspecting the army and recommending improvements. A few years later, in AD 128, Hadrian was in Africa, where he scrutinised the Third Legion as they conducted manoeuvres on the parade ground. Doubtless, he examined the preparations of the British garrison in a similar way. A record of a speech has survived in which he gave an assessment of the soldiers whom he inspected in AD 128:

You did everything in orderly fashion. Your javelin hurling was not without grace. Several of you hurled your lances equally well. And your mounting was smart just now and lively yesterday. If there was anything lacking I should notice it; if there was anything conspicuously bad, I should point it out. But you pleased me uniformly throughout the whole exercise. *(Hadrian)*

Hadrian's visit and the building of the wall prove that he gave a high priority to the security of the province of Britain. Further evidence of the importance of Britain is provided by his decision to send a new legion to Britain and the use of some of his most experienced and effective generals in the province. At the time of his visit, Hadrian appears to have appointed a new governor, Platorius Nepos. He was an old friend of the emperor and had already proved himself in other frontier areas. Nepos took responsibility for the construction of the wall.

The wall was not intended as a single impregnable defence against the northern peoples. It was, rather, part of a bigger system of border defences, and a means of regulating the movement of people in and out of the area of Roman control. The plan evolved as building took place. The original scheme was for a lightly defended wall, with the major garrisons at the rear on the existing military road, the Stanegate. Before the end of Hadrian's reign, the plan had changed and substantial forts were built on the wall itself.

Much of the massive building work was carried out by legionaries from the Second, Sixth and Twentieth Legions and they left official inscriptions commemorating sections of the wall that they had built. Once the building work was done, the legions withdrew to their bases far to the south, while the wall and its forts were manned by auxiliary forces. We do not know what ordinary legionaries felt about their work on the wall. However, some remarkable papyrus letters that have survived in Egypt from about this time give an insight into the attitude of ordinary legionaries towards building work. While most of them undertook heavy labouring, some were exempted because they had other responsibilities. In a letter home written in AD 107 a legionary in Egypt celebrated the fact that he was not required to do building work:

I'm getting on all right. I got here safely, and so far I haven't been caught by any fatigues like cutting building-stones. In fact, I went up to Claudius Severus, the governor, and asked him to make me a clerk. He said, 'I'll make you a clerk of the legion for the time being, with hopes of promotion'. While the others are working hard all day cutting stones, I now stand around doing nothing.

ABOVE *A coin from the reign of Hadrian showing a Roman warship*

BELOW *A nineteenth-century depiction of legionaries at work constructing the wall by William Bell Scott*

SEVERUS AND SONS

RIGHT *The imperial family: Severus, Julia Domna and their two sons. The image of Geta was defaced after his murder by his brother, Caracalla*

ABOVE *A gold coin of Severus. This tough soldier-emperor originated from north Africa and died in York*

ABOVE *The triumphal arch of Severus in Rome. Before his final trip to Britain, Severus had achieved a reputation as a very effective general*

In AD 208 the Emperor Septimius Severus embarked upon a strange mission. He was old and unwell, but he made a long and uncomfortable journey from Rome to Britain. He stayed on the island until his death three years later. Severus had been a very energetic soldier but by the time of his visit to Britain he was no longer able to ride and he was carried all the way from Rome to Britain in a litter. Such was his determination to get to Britain that he refused to stop along the way to rest for any great length of time. Accompanying him were his sons, his wife and a great retinue of courtiers, civil servants, soldiers and lawyers.

Why did Severus go to the obscure province of Britain and stay there until his death? The 'official' justification was that the emperor's presence was a response to renewed unrest on the part of the tribes in Scotland. Roman writers suggest another explanation:

Severus was having difficulty controlling his unruly sons and thought that they would benefit from time spent away from the hothouse atmosphere of Rome itself. The two sons hated each other and both had imperial ambitions. By taking them to Britain, Severus hoped to keep them out of trouble and to groom them for a joint succession to the imperial throne:

> He wanted to get his sons away from Rome so that they might come to their senses amidst the disciplined life of the army, once they were away from the luxury and high life of Rome. For this reason he announced the expedition to Britain, even though he was by now an old man and suffering from gout. *(Herodian)*

Once in Britain, Severus separated his two sons: he took Caracalla with him north on the military campaign, while he left Geta behind in the more settled southern part of the island, with a responsibility for administration and justice. The base for the northern campaign was York and from here Severus continued to run the administration of much of the Empire. Some of the laws he promulgated in Britain have survived, such as one dated 5 May AD 210 and written at York. People from all over the Empire must have travelled to Britain to petition the emperor. We know of an inscription from Ephesus describing how a local man travelled to the extreme west of the Empire to speak to Severus. This may well be a reference to a journey across the whole of Europe to Britain.

Severus and Caracalla took their troops beyond Hadrian's Wall, with the emperor still being carried in a litter. Archaeologists have identified a series of camps from this period in central and eastern Scotland. Skirmishing followed but there was no decisive battle. Some sort of treaty was agreed in AD 209 but the following summer the Britons broke the agreement and took up arms against the Romans. The reaction of Severus was swift and ruthless: he ordered his troops to march north, massacring every British person they met:

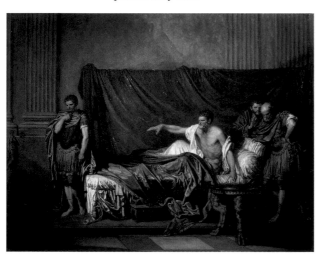

ABOVE *This eighteenth-century history painting, by Jean-Baptiste Greuze, shows Severus accusing his son Caracalla of attempted murder during the campaigns in Scotland. Caracalla was impatient to become emperor and wanted his father out of the way*

When the inhabitants of the island rose again in rebellion, Severus called together his troops and ordered them to invade their territory and to kill everyone they found, and he quoted these lines: 'Let no one escape total destruction at our hands, not even the child carried in its mother's womb'.

Severus was growing increasingly weak and he was obliged to give up active campaigning and remain in York. He told Caracalla to carry on the war on his behalf, but his son had other ideas. Caracalla was more concerned about seizing the imperial crown after his father's death than he was about the defeat of the British barbarians. With his father confined to his quarters, he attempted to persuade the army that he should be their sole leader in the event of his father's death; he might have asked his father's physicians to speed up the emperor's imminent demise:

Caracalla began to persuade the troops to look to him alone for orders, and canvassed for the position of sole ruler in every way that he could, making slanderous attacks against his brother. His father, who had been ill for a long time and was taking his time dying, he regarded as a troublesome nuisance, and he tried to persuade the doctors and attendants to do the old man some injury as they treated him, so that he might be rid of him all the sooner. *(Herodian)*

Severus died in York on 4 February AD 211. According to one of our sources, his death was 'not without a certain amount of help it is said from Caracalla'. Before dying he is supposed to have spoken to both his sons and given them some parting words of advice: 'Live in peace with each other, enrich the army and ignore everyone else.' Caracalla tried to get the army to proclaim him as sole emperor, but the soldiers were not prepared to do this. He abandoned the military campaign and went south to join his brother and mother. Caracalla and Geta then returned to Rome with their father's remains. Their joint rule did not last long. In AD 212 Caracalla murdered Geta.

ABOVE *This coin celebrates the victories of Severus in northern Britain. In reality the emperor failed to consolidate Roman power in Scotland*

THE ARMY OF BRITAIN AND IMPERIAL POLITICS

The Roman emperors depended for their power and position on military might. This gave the legions great political power. Since Britain had one of the largest garrisons in the Empire, it followed that the legions in Britain were particularly powerful. There was an extraordinary example of the clout of the British garrison during the reign of the Emperor Commodus. In AD 182 Commodus appointed a man called Perennis to head up the élite Praetorian guard in Rome. Perennis was given wide powers over the organisation of the army across the Empire.

The troops in Britain were unimpressed by Commodus and Perennis. They attempted to persuade one of their commanders, Priscus, to seize the imperial crown, but Priscus wisely declined. In AD 185 the officers of the British legions decided to protest against Perennis by sending an armed deputation of 1,500 soldiers from Britain to Rome:

> The officers in Britain chose out 1,500 javelin men from their ranks and sent them to Italy. As they drew close to Rome without encountering any resistance, Commodus met them and asked 'What is the meaning of this, my comrades in arms? Why are you here?' They replied, 'We have come because Perennis is plotting against you in order to make his son emperor.'

Commodus completely capitulated to the British deputation. He handed over the unfortunate Perennis and his family to the troops from Britain, who tortured and killed them, before returning to Britain.

A few years later the British forces were again at the centre of imperial politics. The behaviour of the Emperor Commodus became increasingly bizarre, as he began to think that he was the hero Hercules reincarnated, and he was eventually assassinated in AD 192. The death of Commodus led to a bitter civil war, in which the British garrison played a leading part. Three generals, each controlling three legions, claimed the imperial throne. The contenders included Albinus, the governor of Britain. His opponents were Septimius

ABOVE *The Emperor Commodus dressed as Hercules. Troops in Britain marched to Rome to challenge his authority*

Severus on the Danube frontier and Niger in Syria. Of the three, the shrewdest was Severus, who eventually became sole emperor, and he did not underestimate the strength of the British garrison:

> Severus had his suspicions about the forces in Britain. These were large and powerful, and constituted very effective fighters. In command of them was Albinus, a man who by birth belonged to the nobility that made up the Senate, and who had been brought up amidst wealth and inherited luxury. Severus decided to trick him into giving him his support. *(Herodian)*

Severus wrote a flattering letter to Albinus offering joint rule and suggesting that Albinus could become sole ruler one day, since Severus was old and unwell. Albinus believed him, and stayed in Britain while Severus consolidated his position in Rome and defeated the third contender, Niger. By AD 196 Severus felt that he could dispense with Albinus, and he devised a plan to kill him:

> Severus sent for the most trustworthy of his imperial dispatch-carriers and gave them instructions to hand over their dispatches in public, should they be admitted into Albinus' presence, and then to ask him to withdraw in order to hear in greater privacy some secret instructions. If Albinus agreed, they were suddenly to attack and kill him while unprotected by his bodyguards. *(Herodian)*

The plan was not successful, though. Albinus had grown increasingly suspicious of his supposed partner, and tortured the messengers on their arrival and discovered their muderous intentions. Open war then broke out between Albinus, with the backing of British troops, and Severus, who now controlled most of the remaining parts of the Empire. Albinus crossed to Gaul and was finally defeated by Severus at a battle at Lyons in AD 197. It was once thought that the involvement of the British garrison in the fighting in Gaul led to a weakening of the defences in Britain and to incursions from hostile northern tribes. Modern

ABOVE *A coin of Severus. He crushed the British garrison on his road to power*

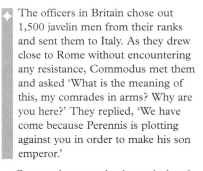

ABOVE *An allegorical relief celebrating the power of Emperor Antoninus Pius. Emperors such as Antoninus were dependent for their position on the goodwill of their armed forces*

force in the Channel. As a result, it was very difficult for Maximian and Diocletian to dislodge him. He adopted the full panoply of imperial power, minting coins showing himself in profile with the other two emperors, with the inscription 'Carausius and his brothers'. His coins also mention legions that were loyal to him, such as the Second and the Twentieth. A milestone found near Carlisle was inscribed with his full 'imperial' name, 'For the Emperor Caesar Marcus Aurelius Musaeus Carausius Pius Felix, the Unconquered Augustus'. For a while Britain function-ed independently of the rest of the Empire. From the perspective of Rome this was a considerable blow to both pride and, perhaps, finances.

archaeologists dispute this theory but believe instead that the energetic military maintenance work begun under the Emperor Severus was motivated by a desire to modernise defences rather than to repair war damage. Although we have no evidence, it seems highly likely that Severus and his new governor of Britain carried out reprisals against those in Britain who had supported Albinus. The usual pattern in such circumstances was that leading sup-porters of the defeated party were put to death and their lands appropriated.

A century later, in AD 287, a usurper called Carausius proclaimed himself emperor in Britain and used the power of the garrison to establish control over the island and part of northern Gaul for a number of years. Carausius was an army officer who had been put in charge of the Roman naval fleet that patrolled the English Channel. This was an important post because shipping was often attacked by Germanic pirates. At this time the Empire was jointly ruled by Maximian and Diocletian. Carausius was an effective military man but a suspicion arose that he was in league with the pirates, and Maximian ordered his execution. Carausius responded by declaring himself emperor, and it seems that he obtained the support of some of the legions in Britain and also the naval

> The loss of Britain was not without significance – a land so rich in harvests, with such abundant pasture, shot through with so many seams of ore, a lucrative source of so much tribute, girded round with so many ports, so vast in its extent.
> *(Panegyric to Constantius, AD 297)*

ABOVE *A reconstruction drawing of the Roman walls being built at Portchester. The fort was probably built at the beginning of Carausius' campaign*

Carausius successfully controlled Britain between AD 286 and 293. In the end he was overthrown, not by the imperial authorities but by Allectus, one of his own men. Allectus then ruled Britain for a further three years before an expeditionary force from Rome finally landed and reasserted Roman power.

THE AGE OF CONSTANTINE

ABOVE *Constantius, the father of Constantine, knew Britain well. This medallion shows him liberating London from the rule of the pretender Allectus in AD 296*

In AD 306 Britain was the setting for one of the most momentous events in the history of Europe. Troops in York proclaimed a young man called Constantine as the new emperor, on the death of his father Constantius. His father was one of the four joint rulers of the Roman Empire (and the second Roman emperor to die in York).

> Seeing, however, that Constantine was a fine figure of a man, and at the same time inspired by hopes of large donations [special payments], the troops invested him with the rank of Caesar.
> *(Zosimus, fifth–sixth centuries AD)*

The acclamation of Constantine was an unconstitutional act. The Emperor Diocletian (ruled AD 284–305) had tried to establish a new system for determining the imperial succession. He had divided the Empire into western and eastern halves and created a senior and junior emperor in each area. Under these rules, Constantius should have been succeeded by a man called Severus, who was the junior emperor in the west, but the troops in York thought differently. Constantine's bid for control of the Empire was opposed by powerful enemies and it was only after eighteen years of struggle and civil war that he eventually became the undisputed ruler of the Roman Empire. As emperor he legalised and encouraged the Christian faith, thereby helping to shape the future of medieval Europe. He also founded a great new capital at Byzantium, which he renamed Constantinople (known today as Istanbul). Constantine did not forget Britain; he talked about the divine mission that had led him from his accession in Britain, on the western

ABOVE *Constantine had a major impact on European history because of his decision to embrace Catholic Christianity. This medieval fresco shows him and Pope Sylvester*

ABOVE *A wall-painting from a Roman villa in Trier. Workers toil in the field against the backdrop of a villa. The early fourth century was a period of prosperity in the countryside*

edge of the world, to Constantinople in the far east of the Roman Empire. He also proudly styled himself 'Britannicus Maximus'. The court poet Eumenius celebrated Britain's role as the place where Constantine began his imperial career in gushing tones. His account suggests that Britain was still seen, at this late date, as a mysterious place on the edge of the known world:

> Fortunate and happier than all lands, because she first saw Constantine as Caesar. Gracious gods! What means this, that always from some remote end of the world new deities descend to be universally revered? Truly places nearer to heaven are more sacred than inland regions; and it was very proper that an emperor should be sent by the gods from the region where the earth terminates. *(Eumenius, fourth century AD)*

The reign of Constantine coincided with a period of prosperity in the Romanised parts of rural Britain.

The most clear-cut evidence of this lies in the proliferation of villas during the first half of the fourth century AD. Some of these villas were extremely small, suggesting that the Romanised lifestyle was appealing to a greater section of British society. Very grand villas were also being built, as at Woodchester, and earlier villas were being remodelled on a magnificent scale, as at Bignor and Chedworth. This period also saw a flowering of the mosaicist's art, particularly in the south-central and south-west regions, and many of the finest mosaics were found in villas. The palatial villa at Woodchester in Gloucestershire possesses the largest known mosaic floor in north-west Europe. There was also, despite the Christian leanings of the emperor, a growth in the number of pagan temples in the countryside. These were, presumably, paid for by the same self-confident class that built the contemporary villas. It seems that there was a substantial élite of wealthy Romanised people who felt confident about the future and chose to invest in prestigious rural buildings.

While the ruling class seems to have enjoyed prosperity in the countryside, there were some puzzling changes in the towns of late Roman Britain. The largest towns seem to have declined in significance, and after the second century, few major public buildings were erected. At Silchester, for example, the basilica fell into disuse in the third century. At the same time the towns were not impoverished: some very fine town houses were built in the early fourth century, similar in style to the rural villas of the same period. It seems that the élite of Roman Britain felt little responsibility for the upkeep of public buildings in the towns but continued to maintain and develop residential properties in the towns. There was less evidence of the energetic economic activity of the first centuries. Much of the province's industrial enterprise transferred to the countryside and to smaller towns. Some archaeologists have described the major towns of the early fourth century as 'garden cities', quiet places with fine houses and a semi-rural quality.

The reigns of Diocletian and Constantine were marked by significant changes in the way the imperial army

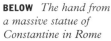

was organised. Britain was not at the forefront of the struggles between Rome and her barbarian enemies in the third and early fourth centuries, and the size of the British garrison was accordingly reduced. In AD 150 there was a force of about 50,000 troops in Britain; the garrison was probably only half that size in the early fourth century. In the second century the British army represented about twelve per cent of the total Roman army, but this had fallen to about five per cent in the fourth century. The British garrison was not only smaller, it was structured in a different way. Instead of legionaries and auxiliaries, a new distinction was made between second-class troops known as 'limitanei', and an élite mobile field army, called 'comitatenses'. We know from a later document that at about this time a new official appeared at York called 'Dux Britanniarum' – the leader of the Britons. This individual probably co-ordinated the activities of both the border troops and those detachments of the élite field army that were operating in northern Britain.

PAGANS AND CHRISTIANS

ABOVE *During the Roman period many religions from the eastern Mediterranean were brought to Britain. One was the worship of Mithras, seen here in a carving found at Housesteads*

BELOW *A bronze figure of the god Mercury from Richborough. Christianity only began to challenge the worship of pagan gods in Britain during the fourth century AD*

C hristianity was one of several religions that spread from the eastern Mediterranean to Britain during the Roman period. London, as a cosmopolitan port, was a place where many exotic faiths were practised. There is evidence, for example, from London of devotion to the Egyptian goddess, Isis. A flagon found in Southwark was inscribed in Latin: 'London, at the temple of Isis'. London also possessed a temple to Mithras; the men-only cult of the god Mithras, originating far away in Iran, was popular among soldiers. There was also a temple to Mithras at Carrawburgh in Northumberland. The army also took some eastern cults to other parts of the province. A temple to the Egyptian deity Serapis-Osiris was built in York by a commander of the resident Sixth Legion. On Hadrian's Wall there is substantial evidence of the garrison's devotion to Mithras, such as this inscription from Housesteads:

> To the Unconquered Sun Mithras, Lord of Ages, Litorius Pacatanius, seconded for special duty by the governor, willingly and deservedly fulfilled his vow.

We know very little about how Christianity reached Britain. Like the other eastern religions, it was probably introduced into the province by visiting merchants or soldiers. It does not seem that there was a very large Christian presence in Britain before the fourth century. The earliest reference to the Christians of Britain comes from about AD 200, when the Christian writer Tertullian described how there were 'places in Britain inaccessible to the Romans, but which have submitted to Christ'.

Throughout the Empire, Christianity was sporadically persecuted before the edict of AD 313, by which Constantine legalised the faith. We have the names of three Christians who were put to death in Britain for their faith before the legalisation of Christianity. Alban was killed outside Verulamium, and he is famous for being the first British saint and martyr. The modern town of St Albans is, of course, named after him. Less well-known are the two Christians who were martyred in Caerleon in south Wales. Their names are recorded as Julius and Aaron – the latter name is intriguing because it is Jewish.

As soon as Constantine made possible public expression of Christianity, British Christians stepped out of the shadows. In AD 314, a year after the religion became tolerated, a church council was held at Arles in Gaul and British delegates were listed as being present:

> Eborius, bishop of the city of York in the province of Britain, Restitutus, bishop of the city of London in the above-mentioned province, Adelphius bishop of the city Colonia Londonensium [a scribe has made an error here, this may refer to Lincoln 'Colonia Lindinensium'], also Sacerdus, presbyter, and Arminius, deacon. *(Acts of the Council of Arles, AD 314)*

Sulpicius Severus writing in the fifth century AD described how impoverished British delegates attended another church council held at Rimini in AD 359.

ABOVE *The Christian 'chi-rho' symbol from a hoard of Christian vessels and wall decorations found at Water Newton*

ABOVE *A reconstruction drawing of a baptism at Richborough. Merchants and soldiers might have brought Christianity to Britain*

BELOW *A Bacchanalian scene from the magnificent Mildenhall Treasure*

The most common Christian symbol of the Roman years was the so-called 'chi-rho', a sign based on the two Greek letters which were the first two letters of the word 'Christos'. At the villa at Hinton St Mary in Dorset a fourth-century Christian mosaic showed a Christ-like figure against the background of the 'chi-rho' sign, and flanked with pomegranates – a Christian symbol of eternal life. There arc many examples of the 'chi-rho' sign on the rich collection of Christian sacred vessels and wall-plaques, found at Water Newton in 1975. This collection appears to have been hidden in the middle of the fourth century. Sometimes Christian and pagan symbolism existed side by side. One of the great collections in the British Museum is the Mildenhall Treasure of fourth-century decorated vessels, which included both magnificent pagan vessels, showing scenes of wild Bacchanalian celebration and spoons inscribed with the 'chi-rho' sign.

It is difficult to be certain about the level of popularity of Christianity in Roman Britain. We know very little about the extent of the faith before the age of Constantine. A few fourth-century buildings in towns have been identified as probable churches at Silchester, Canterbury and St Albans. Possible churches have also been identified at forts such as Richborough and Vindolanda. More clear-cut proof of a Roman church comes from Lullingstone Villa, where a chapel was established in the fourth century. It was decorated with wall-paintings, showing people standing at prayer with their arms outstretched.

It is possible that some pagan temples might have been reused as Christian places of worship. At the temple to Mithras in London the pagan sculpture was dismantled in the middle of the fourth century and buried. At a small possible church site at Icklingham in Suffolk, pagan items were buried in a pit. Deliberately damaged pagan altars were reused at a Christian site at Uley temple in Gloucestershire. At Chedworth a shrine centred on a spring might have been converted into a baptismal tank in the late fourth century. The slabs at the edge of the basin were inscribed with the 'chi-rho' sign. There are occasional hints of the conflict that must have taken place between Christians and pagans. At Bath a centurion called Gaius Severius Emeritus installed an altar as part of the rededication of the temple after an act of vandalism. He described how 'this holy spot' had been 'wrecked by insolent hands'. This may be a reference to Christian attacks on the great pagan centre at Bath.

ABOVE *The inhabitants of Lullingstone Villa in the fourth century AD were Christian. The restored paintings of praying figures and Christian symbols can be seen at the British Museum. One scholar has suggested that the villa might have been used as a monastery*

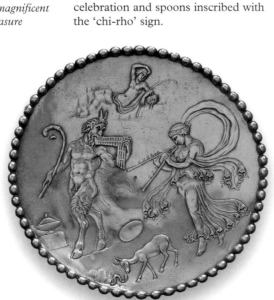

THE GATHERING STORM

ABOVE *Two skeletons were found in a London cemetery, buried with Germanic-style grave goods. This reconstruction drawing gives an idea of what they must once have looked like*

What did the most powerful people in the Roman Empire think about Britain in the fourth century AD? Some of the Empire's wealthiest people owned estates in Britain as absentee landlords: we know that a wealthy Christian lady called Melania owned land in Britain, as well as in Italy, north Africa and Spain. Despite these connections, Britain was still seen as a remote place on the edge of the world. Visits to Britain were not always voluntary; we know that on occasion, Britain, like other islands, was used as a place of exile for disgraced members of the ruling class.

> A certain Valentinus, a haughty character born in Valeria in Pannonia, had been exiled to Britain because of a serious crime. Like a dangerous animal he could not bear to be inactive and he stirred himself to acts of wickedness and revolution.
> *(Ammianus Marcellinus)*

Valentinus continued his scheming while in Britain and was discreetly put to death by the imperial authorities.

A poem written by Ausonius, an influential and aristocratic writer from Gaul, in about AD 382 suggests that the British were viewed contemptuously by some. He attacks an otherwise unknown Briton called Silvius Bonus. The second name of the British poet means 'good' and Ausonius had much fun at his expense by suggesting that it was a contradiction in terms to link any British person to the word 'good':

> 'This is Silvius Good.'
> 'Who is Silvius?'
> 'He is a Briton.'
> 'Either this Silvius is no Briton,
>   or he is Silvius Bad.'
> 'Silvius is called Good and called a
>   Briton: who would believe a good
>   citizen had sunk so low? No good
>   man is a Briton.'   *(Ausonius)*

Occasionally events in Britain played an important part in overall imperial politics. Compared to the rest of the Empire, Britain was relatively immune from the impact of barbarian incursions in the third century. The first half of the fourth century was also a time of apparent peace in Britain. However, in about AD 367 Roman Britain was attacked simultaneously by several hostile armies in the so-called 'barbarian conspiracy'. Our chief source for this incident, the historian Ammianus Marcellinus, described how news of the crisis in Britain reached the horrified Emperor Valentinian in Gaul:

> Valentinian had set out from Amiens and was hurrying towards Trier when he was overtaken by grave reports indicating that Britain had been plunged into the depths of distress by a conspiracy of the barbarians, that Nectaridus, count of the coastal district, had been killed, and the Duke Fullofaudes had been surrounded and captured in an enemy ambush. This news was received with great consternation. *(Ammianus Marcellinus)*

According to Ammianus, the situation in Britain was catastrophic, with leading imperial officers killed or captive. He explained how 'marauding enemy bands… were roaming about, loaded down with the weight of their booty and… driving along prisoners and cattle'. Eventually a high-ranking official called Count Theodosius was sent to restore order. The son of Theodosius was later to become emperor and the historian Ammianus is suspected of writing an account of the barbarian conspiracy intended to glorify the deeds of the emperor's father. Theodosius landed at Richborough with a large armed force and marched towards London, and as he moved through Kent he dispersed the barbarians and restored stolen goods to grateful owners. Theodosius paused in London, interrogated freed prisoners, and declared an amnesty for deserters from the army. He then moved on to pacify the rest of Britain. Another Roman historian called Claudian celebrated, and probably massively exaggerated, the carnage among the repulsed barbarian tribes:

> What profit to the Britons the eternal harshness and cold of their climate, or the uncharted seas? The Orkneys were drenched with the slaughter of Saxons; Thule was warm with Pictish blood, and icy Ireland wept for heaps of Scottish dead.
> *(Claudian, late fourth century)*

ABOVE *A Germanic-style belt set of the late fourth to early fifth century AD found in a burial in London*

ABOVE *The coastal fort at Portchester in the mid-fourth century* AD*. Britain was spared much of the chaos that took place on the Continent during the fourth century* AD *but in* AD 367 *the province was convulsed by the so-called barbarian conspiracy*

Modern archaeologists believe that we should be sceptical about these literary descriptions of chaos and slaughter. There is little archaeological evidence suggestive of great disruption caused by barbarian invaders.

By the late fourth century AD the size of the British garrison of the Roman army was greatly reduced compared to the earlier years of Roman rule. In some parts of the Empire Germanic units were deployed by the Roman authorities to strengthen the army. There is no convincing evidence for the use of barbarian mercenaries in fourth-century Britain. It seems that Britain was still considered to be a relatively secure area, not in need of barbarian reinforcement. In AD 383 Magnus Maximus, a leading Roman officer based in Britain, was proclaimed as emperor by the troops of the British garrison. This was, of course, only the latest instance in a long line of examples of the soldiers in Britain flexing their muscles and intefering in high imperial politics. One Roman writer said of this episode that the soldiers in Britain 'were steeped more than all others in surliness and anger'. Maximus crossed to Gaul with his supporters and took the Emperor Gratian by surprise:

Maximus, a man vigorous in action, upright and worthy of imperial honours had he not risen to prominence by breaking his oath of loyalty and an illegal assumption of power, was created emperor by the army in Britain almost against his will. He then crossed to Gaul. There he treacherously surrounded and killed the Emperor Gratian, who was terrified by this sudden attack and was considering crossing into Italy. *(Orosius)*

Maximus continued to rule Britain, Gaul and Spain for five years before he was overthrown and killed by the Emperor Theodosius, son of the man who had rescued Britain from the barbarian conspiracy.

ABOVE *A reconstruction drawing showing the Roman coastal station at Scarborough with raiders landing*

LEFT *The Hoxne hoard. Treasure was often hidden in uncertain times*

THE END OF ROMAN RULE

ABOVE *The history of Britain after the end of Roman rule is shrouded in mystery. This tombstone from Wroxeter sheds a little light. It dates from 450–75 AD and commemorates a man called 'Cunorix', the hound king. He seems to have been an Irish chieftain who was based in the former Roman town*

The early years of the fifth century were a time of great crisis for the Roman Empire. In AD 407, while hostile tribes threatened Gaul and Italy, the Roman garrison in Britain attempted to place a series of new emperors on the imperial throne:

> The soldiers in Britain rebelled, elevated Marcus to the imperial throne and gave him their obedience as ruler there. However, because he was not in tune with their ways, they put him to death, and promoted Gratian, granting him a bodyguard as they would an emperor. However, not finding him to their liking either, they deposed him and put him to death after four months and gave the throne to Constantine.   *(Zosimus)*

This third usurper, calling himself Constantine III, crossed to Gaul, with forces from Britain, and tried to take control of the western half of the Empire. The landed aristocracy of Roman Britain was probably unimpressed by these developments and by the departure of part of the defensive army to take part in Constantine's bid for power. The crisis in the Empire had led to a great increase in taxation and this was another reason for discontent among the landowning class in Britain. When between AD 408 and 409 Britain was attacked by barbarians, the leaders of British society showed their exasperation by breaking away from imperial authority and taking charge of their own affairs:

> Since Constantine failed to resist this attack, the barbarians across the Rhine attacked everywhere with all their strength, and brought the people of Britain to the point where they revolted from Roman rule and lived by themselves, no longer obeying Roman rules.   *(Zosimus)*

As a result of the revolt of AD 409 Britain was no longer ruled as an integral part of the Roman Empire. The Emperor Honorius, from his base at Ravenna in northern Italy, could do little to alter this state of affairs and in AD 410 he wrote to the cities of Britain telling them that they could expect no military help from him and must look to their own defences. Shipments of coins as payment for the military stopped and, as a result, the circulation of new money came to an abrupt end. Without money, parts of the economy collapsed and the most dramatic evidence for this is the way in which the large-scale production of pottery rapidly ceased.

The life of St Patrick gives some insight into the unsettled conditions in the aftermath of the separation of Britain from the Empire. Patrick came from a Romanised Christian landowning family and he was brought up somewhere in the west of Britain. He was kidnapped and taken to Ireland by a band of pirates at the age of sixteen. He later recalled this incident in his autobiography:

ABOVE *A reconstruction drawing of Wroxeter in the fifth century AD*

> I, Patrick, the lowest and least of all the faithful, the most contemptible of many, had as my father Calpornius, a deacon and son of the priest, Potius who lived in the village of Bannavem Taburniae. He had a small estate nearby and there I was taken prisoner. I was then about sixteen.
> *(St Patrick, fifth century AD)*

We do not know what happened to any remaining units of the Roman army that might have been in Britain after about AD 409. Some might have been employed by chieftains, who probably filled the power vacuum created by the break with Rome. Writing in the sixth century, a British monk called Gildas talked disparagingly about the 'tyrants' who ruled over

BELOW *This nineteenth-century painting by Thomas Couture shows the traditional view of the decadent Romans who were responsible for the decline and fall of the Empire. There is little evidence from Britain to support this view. Roman Britain remained prosperous and stable for most of the fourth century AD*

different areas of Britain after the end of Roman authority. Although he was writing more than a century later, and his work is notoriously puzzling and unreliable, the account of Gildas gives some sense of the antagonism towards the 'barbarian' people felt by Romanised Britons:

> And so, as the Romans returned home, the loathsome hordes of Scots and Picts eagerly emerged from the coracles that carried them across the gulf of the sea, like dark swarms of worms that emerge from their holes when the sun is high and the weather grows warm. In custom they differed slightly one from another, yet in their single desire for shedding blood they were of one accord.
> *(Gildas, sixth century AD)*

Urban life, which had already been in decline before AD 400, continued to wither. There was very little further building in stone. For a while, after AD 410, some urban authorities appear to have remained functioning. Excavations have shown that at St Albans the aqueduct was kept in working order, and street surfaces were maintained in Winchester. However, within a few decades, towns had largely ceased to function as administrative and economic centres. Some towns such as Wroxeter in Shropshire might have continued as the headquarters for powerful local chieftains.

During the fifth century there was a gradual settlement of Germanic Anglo-Saxon people in the east of Britain. As they moved west the Saxons displaced the Romanised landowning class and imposed their language and pagan religious beliefs on the people. There was no mass slaughter of the inhabitants: the common people remained but they had new masters. The spread of Saxon power was slow and uneven; according to the *Anglo-Saxon Chronicle* the Saxons did not control Bath, Cirencester and Gloucester until after a battle in AD 577. The south-eastern portion of Roman 'Britannia' was slowly transformed into 'England', the land of the Angles and Saxons.

BELOW *Bracelets from the Hoxne treasure. These items were buried in the unsettled conditions of the early fifth century AD*

59

THE ROMAN LEGACY

Although the Empire in western Europe collapsed in the fifth century, the Romans' achievements have continued to influence politics, culture and scholarship. Until very recently a grounding in Latin literature and Classical history was considered to be an essential element of a good education. Our grammar schools are so called because they were established for the study of Latin grammar and literature. Latin was, for many centuries after the fall of Rome, the international language of scholarship and science. This is still reflected today in the use of Latin to provide a technical terminology in subjects such as botany and anatomy.

The Romans were renowned for their political authority and as different

CENTRE *Chiswick House in London. Its builders aimed to return to the principles of Roman architecture*

ABOVE *A Roman mosaic showing the writer Virgil and two muses. The study of Roman writers such as Virgil had a central place in the school curriculum until recent times*

routinely use when describing the law are taken from the vocabulary of the Roman world: 'magistrate', 'tribunal', 'justice' and 'legal'. The Catholic Church is a modern institution that can trace its origins to the world of the Roman Empire. The pope is also known as the pontiff, a term derived from the Latin 'pontifex maximus', used by the chief priest in pagan times, and given to the pope as bishop of Rome when the Empire became Christian.

In Britain, traces of our Roman past surround us. Our months of the year are based on the Roman months: in July and August we still commemorate the great Roman rulers, Julius Caesar and Augustus. The pattern of Roman roads continues to influence the shape of the modern road network. It is still possible to travel, as the Romans did, along the Fosse Way from Cirencester to Leicester. Many of the cities and towns of modern Britain are based on Roman foundations: places such as Bath, Gloucester, Chester, York, Exeter and, greatest of all both then and now, London. The layout of the streets in these places is often based on the topography of the Roman town. A few Roman towns did not develop into flourishing modern settlements, such as Wroxeter and Silchester, and they provide, instead, a rich archaeological heritage to modern excavators.

Our language is full of other words derived from Latin. It is wrong to think that this linguistic heritage is a direct consequence of the Roman occupation of Britain. After the ending of Roman control and the advent of Anglo-Saxon migrants, the people of England spoke a Germanic language. In the western Mediterranean countries, Latin continued in use and eventually evolved into the modern 'Romance' languages of French, Spanish

RIGHT *The story of Rome and its fall continued to pre-occupy people for many centuries. This painting by Pannini dates from 1757 and shows the Colosseum in a ruinous landscape with an allegory of the fall of Rome*

people have sought to establish new political systems they have looked back to the Romans for inspiration and for some reflected glory. The Russians called their kings 'czars', the Germans 'kaisers'; in both cases the word was based on Caesar, the name of the Roman emperors. Similarly, the founders of the United States of America sought to give their new constitution dignity and authority by naming the upper house of their legislature the Senate. One of the Romans' great contributions to the world was their attempt to establish a systematic and rational legal system. In much of Europe modern legal systems are still based on the principles of Roman law. Many of the words we

BELOW *A fifteenth-century manuscript of the* Lives of the Caesars *by Suetonius. People have remained fascinated by the rulers of Ancient Rome. The German 'kaiser' and the Russian 'czar' saw themselves literally as latter-day caesars*

and Italian. This did not happen in England, but French-speaking Normans brought many Latinate words to England after 1066.

Architecture has been greatly influenced by the styles used by the Romans. Anglo-Saxons and Normans built their great churches in a so-called Romanesque style, based on the traditions of Rome. There was a great revival of the Classical styles of architecture, based on the legacy of Ancient Greece and Rome. Between 1600 and 1900 most public buildings in Britain and the rest of Europe were built in a consciously Classical style. Appropriately, the great Roman city of Bath was reshaped in the eighteenth century by architects using Classical ideas derived from the architecture of Ancient Rome.

The people of Britain and Europe have never forgotten their Roman legacy. Throughout the Middle Ages, Roman and Greek writers were seen as the most authoritative sources of knowledge. The study of medicine, for example, was dominated for over a thousand years by the writings of a doctor called Galen, who worked in the Roman Empire. When, in the fifteenth and sixteenth centuries, there was a 'rebirth' or Renaissance in art and learning, artists and scholars modelled themselves on their predecessors in the world of Classical Antiquity. Interest in Rome remains strong today, as is evidenced by the number of visitors who go to important Roman sites such as the Roman baths complex at Bath and the extant remains of Hadrian's Wall.

A sense of awe at the achievements of the people who lived in Roman Britain was articulated long ago by an anonymous Anglo-Saxon writer of the eighth century. He looked at the substantial remains of a Roman settlement, quite possibly at Bath, and marvelled at the skill of its builders:

ABOVE *A drawing of Roman lettering from Ivy Chimneys in Essex. Our alphabet is derived from the one used by the Romans*

Wondrous is this masonry shattered by the Fates. The fortifications have given way, the buildings raised by giants are crumbling. The roofs have collapsed; the towers are in ruins… This wall has outlasted kingdom after kingdom, standing unmoved by storms. The lofty arch has fallen… There were splendid palaces and many halls with water flowing through them; a wealth of gables towered aloft. And so these courts lie desolate, and the framework of the dome with its red arches sheds its tiles… where of old many a warrior, joyous hearted and radiant with gold, shone resplendent in the harness of battle, proud and flushed with wine. He gazed upon the treasure, the silver, the precious stones, upon wealth, riches and pearls, upon this splendid citadel. There stood courts of stone, and a stream gushed forth in rippling floods of hot water.
(Anglo-Saxon writer, eighth century)

ABOVE Spring *by Sir Lawrence Alma-Tadema. This Victorian painter, like the Anglo-Saxon poet who wrote 'The Ruin', looked back admiringly to the extraordinary world of Ancient Rome*

WHAT TO SEE TODAY

⚓ ALDBOROUGH, North Yorkshire. Once the site of a Roman town and a tribal centre for the Brigantes people. Remains of town defences and mosaics. Small museum with Roman finds.

ANTONINE WALL. This once stretched from the Firth of Clyde in the west to the Firth of Forth in the east. A few sections of the bank and ditch are still visible, most notably at Watling Dyke and Rough Castle in Stirlingshire. There are also some excavated and displayed buildings at Bearsden in Glasgow.

BAGINTON, Warwickshire. The remains of a first-century fort. The east gateway and part of the ramparts have been reconstructed.

BATH, Avon. Major Roman religious centre built around the town's sacred spring. Extensive Roman remains, including the Great Bath and a suite of other baths. Major collection of Roman finds on display.

BIGNOR, West Sussex. Elaborate villa dating largely to the fourth century, including some fine mosaics.

BINCHESTER, County Durham. Parts of a fort, and the remains of a bath house, complete with hypocaust.

BRADING VILLA, Isle of Wight. This Roman villa still has some fine mosaics, including one of Orpheus, and another of Perseus and Andromeda.

BRECON GAER, Wales. The remains of a fort, which lay at the junction of several roads.

⚓ BURGH CASTLE, Norfolk. Impressive walls of a late third-century fort.

BURNSWARK, Dumfriesshire. An Iron Age hillfort with impressive ramparts, surrounded by Roman siege camps.

CAER GYBI, Holyhead, Wales. The remains of a bridge head fortification with defensive walls.

CAERLEON *(above right)*, Wales. Remains of a legionary fort. Base for the Second Legion. Substantial remains include amphitheatre, barrack blocks and baths.

CAERNARFON, Wales. The foundations of the Roman fort, Segontium.

CAERWENT, Wales. Once the tribal centre for the Silures people. Remains of

the Roman town, including the best-preserved town defences in Britain.

⚓ CAISTER ROMAN SITE, Norfolk. Roman fort with surviving wall and gateway.

CARDIFF, Wales. Roman collection at the National Museum of Wales.

CAWTHORN, North Yorkshire. Traces of Roman camps.

CHEDWORTH, Gloucestershire. A villa with baths and fine mosaics.

⚓ CHESTER, Cheshire. Legionary fortress and home to the Twentieth Legion. Remains of an amphitheatre. Roman collection at the Grosvenor Museum.

CHEW GREEN CAMP, Northumberland. The remains of a marching and siege camp, set in spectacular scenery.

⚓ CIRENCESTER, Gloucestershire. Amphitheatre and traces of town walls. Large Roman collection, including local mosaics in the town's Corinium Museum.

COLCHESTER, Essex. Remains of town walls and gateways. Norman castle built on the base of the massive temple to Claudius and scene of fierce fighting during the rebellion of Boudicca. The Castle Museum has an important Roman collection.

DORCHESTER, Dorset. The remains of a Roman town house in Colliton Park, and the remains of an amphitheatre, known as Maumbury Rings.

⚓ DOVER CASTLE, Kent. Roman lighthouse in the middle of the medieval castle.

FISHBOURNE, West Sussex. Large villa or palace with mosaics and a restored Roman garden.

⚓ GREAT WITCOMBE, Gloucestershire. Substantial Roman villa.

HADRIAN'S WALL
The most impressive remains from Roman Britain are to be found along the wall. The best remains of the wall itself are to be found in the central section. There are a number of important sites and museums associated with the wall:

⚓ BIRDOSWALD. Fort with gates and granaries, and nearby extensive remains of the Wall.

CARRAWBURGH *(above)*. This fort is in private ownership, but nearby is the temple to Mithras which is open to the public.

CARVORAN ROMAN ARMY MUSEUM. Exhibitions relating to the Roman army in northern Britain.

⚓ CHESTERS FORT AND MUSEUM. Remains of fort including substantial bath-house, with a changing-room and a suite of different baths. Important Roman collection in the museum. Nearby are the remains of a massive masonry bridge across the River Tyne.

⚓ CORBRIDGE ROMAN SITE. Remains of military supply base and adjacent civilian site, including granaries, military buildings and museum.

⌗ HOUSESTEADS FORT (below left). Best-preserved of the forts on the Wall. Extensive remains include latrines, headquarters building, commandant's house, barracks and defences. Small museum.

NEWCASTLE MUSEUM OF ANTIQUITIES. Major Roman collection including reconstruction of Temple to Mithras.

SOUTH SHIELDS FORT AND MUSEUM. Built to protect shipping entering the mouth of the Tyne. Remains of granaries from Roman fort. Museum containing the tombstone of Regina (see page six).

TULLIE HOUSE MUSEUM, Carlisle. Roman collection from sites at the western end of the Wall.

⌗ VINDOLANDA (Chesterholm). Remains of fort and adjacent 'vicus' or civilian settlement. The remarkable Vindolanda letters have been found here during recent decades (see page thirty-two).

WALLSEND ROMAN FORT. Extreme east end of the Wall. From 2000, the whole fort plan will be visible, plus a stretch of the Wall. There is also a museum.

HARDKNOTT ROMAN FORT, Cumbria. The remains of a fort that controlled the road from Ravenglass to Ambleside, and, nearby, the remains of a bath house and parade ground.

HIGH ROCHESTER, Northumberland. The remains of a fort, plus traces of a mausoleum. Nearby is an open-air museum of simulated buildings.

HOD HILL, Dorset. The remains of a Roman fort in the corner of a prehistoric hillfort.

LEICESTER. Remains of the great baths adjacent to the Jewry Wall Museum, with its Roman collection.

LINCOLN. Gates and basilica wall visible. Roman collection in museum.

LONDON. Major Roman collections at both the British Museum and the Museum of London. Remains of town wall and wall walk near the Museum of London. Reconstructed Temple of Mithras at Temple Court, Queen Victoria Street.

⌗ LULLINGSTONE, Kent. Villa with fine mosaics and bath suite. Remains of underfloor heating system. Evidence of Christian ownership.

LYMPNE SAXON SHORE FORT, Kent. The remains of the shore fort, known as Portus Lemanis, including some large sections of wall.

⌗ MAIDEN CASTLE, Dorset. Iron Age hillfort that was attacked during the early stages of the Roman conquest. Foundations of a Roman temple at the centre of the hillfort.

NEWPORT VILLA, Isle of Wight. This Roman villa has a well-preserved bath suite, including a plunge bath and the remains of a hypocaust system.

⌗ NORTH LEIGH, Oxfordshire. Villa with fine geometric patterned mosaic.

⌗ PEVENSEY CASTLE, Sussex. Roman shore fort and later medieval remains.

⌗ PIERCEBRIDGE ROMAN BRIDGE, North Yorkshire. The remains of the stone piers and abutment of a Roman timber bridge over the River Tees.

⌗ PORTCHESTER, Hampshire. Situated on Portsmouth harbour, this was a fortified base for the Roman fleet. Impressive remains of the Roman walls and later Norman castle.

⌗ RECULVER, Kent. The remains of a Roman fort, standing in a country park.

⌗ RICHBOROUGH (above), Kent. Now some distance from the sea, this was once an extremely busy Roman port. Massive walls and ditches remain from the later period of Roman occupation.

ROCKBOURNE VILLA, Hampshire. The remains of a Roman villa, with some mosaics. There is also a small museum.

ST ALBANS, Hertfordshire. Roman Verulamium, tribal capital of the Catuvellauni people. Traditional site of the death of the first British Christian martyr, Alban. Remains of walls, theatre and houses. Important Roman collection in the town's Verulamium Museum.

⌗ SCARBOROUGH, North Yorkshire. The site of a fourth-century Roman signal station, just by the castle.

SENHOUSE MUSEUM, Maryport, Cumbria. This museum contains an impressive set of Roman altars.

⌗ SILCHESTER, Hampshire. The best-preserved Roman town walls in Britain, with an impressive amphitheatre. Finds from the excavation are displayed at Reading Museum.

⌗ WALL, Staffordshire. Small Roman settlement on Watling Street. Remains of a bath-house and roadside 'mansio' or guesthouse.

⌗ WHEELDALE ROMAN ROAD, North Yorkshire. A mile-long stretch of Roman road which runs across isolated moorland.

WOODCHESTER, Gloucestershire. This villa possesses the largest known mosaic floor in north-west Europe.

⌗ WROXETER (above), Shropshire. Tribal centre for the Cornovii people. Impressive remains of the baths basilica.

YORK. Legionary fortress. Used as a base by Severus during his stay in Britain, and the place where Constantine was proclaimed emperor. Remains of Roman defences, and an important collection in the town's Castle Museum. Roman foundations are still visible below York Minster.

⌗ Sites in the care of English Heritage. Telephone 01793-414910 for details.

INDEX

abatons 21
administration 8, 26–7, 34–5
Agricola 8, 18, 29, 44–5
Alban, Saint 54
Albinus 50–1
Allectus 51, *52*
alumni 11
amphitheatres 8, 9, 17
amphorae 14, *14*
Anglesey 45
Anglo-Saxons 59, 60, 61
Antonine Itinerary 12
Antonine Wall 14
Antoninus Pius, Emperor 8, *50*
aqueducts 59
army 10, 17, 26–35, *26–31*, 31, *33*, 37, *45*, 50–1, 53
Auchendavy 14
Augustus, Emperor 12, 35, 60
auxiliaries 27, 28, 29, 30, 31, *31*, 32, 41, *45*

Barates 6–7, *6*
barbarian conspiracy 56–7
basilicas 8, 17, *35*
Batavians 29, 32
Bath 11, 12, 16, 21, *21*, 22–3, *23*, 27, 55, 59, 61
bath-houses *4–5*, 6, 8, 9, 16–17, *16*, 19
beer 15, 33
Benwell *21*
Bignor 53
Bishopsgate *25*
Boudicca 8, 9, 26, 28, 43, *43*, 44
Brigantians 42
Britannia 9, *34*, *40*
burial 24–5
Byzantium 52

Caerleon 12, 17, *17*, 24–5, 27, 54
Caesar, Julius 10, 14, 20, 38–9, *38*, *39*, 40, 41, 60
Caledonia 29, 37, 45
Calgacus 45
Camulodunum *see* Colchester
Canterbury 17, *17*, 55, *59*
Caracalla 48–9, *48*, *49*
Caratacus 41, 42
Carausius 51
Carlisle 51
Carrawburgh 54
Cartimandua 42
Cassius, Dio 37, 40, 41, 43
Catus, Decianus 26, 43
Catuvellaunians 6, 7, 40–1
cavalry 27, *29*, 30
Celts 6, 7, 20–1, *20*, *21*, 22, 33, *38*, 41
cemeteries 24
centurions 32
Charterhouse 15
Chedworth 53, *53*, 55
Chester 11, 27, *28*, 60

Christianity 19, 53, 54–5, *54*, *55*, 58
Cicero 10, 36, 39
Cirencester 24, 59, 60
citizenship, Roman 27, 28, 31
civitates 8
Claudian 15, 56
Claudius, Emperor 12–13, 28, 40–1, *40*, *41*, 42–3
clothing 7, *15*, 31, 45, *56*
Cogidumnus 42
coins *34*, 37, 38, 39, 41, *41*, *42*, *47*, 48, 49, 50, 57
coloniae 8, 9, 27
Colosseum 60
comitatenses 53
Commodus, Emperor 50, *50*
Compton Dando 23
Constans, Emperor 13
Constantine III 58
Constantine, Emperor 13, 52–3, *52*, *53*, 55
Constantius 51, 52
Corbridge *23*, *28*, *32*
Cornovii 9
Coventina's Well 21
cremation 24, *25*
Cripplegate 9
Cunobelinus 40–1, 42
curiales 8
cursus publicus 12–13
customs 13
Cymbeline *see* Cunobelinus

death 24–5
decurions 8
Desborough *37*
diet 13, 17, 18, 33
Diocletian, Emperor 15, 51, 52, 53
divination 22
divorce 36
Dolaucothi 15
Domitian, Emperor 34, 45
Dorchester 25, *25*
Dover *13*, 15
dress 7
druids 20–1, *20*
Dumnonii 17
duplicarius 30
Durobrivae *see* Water Newton
Dux Britanniarum 53

East Coker 16
education 36–7, *44*, 45, 60, *60*
equestrian officers 27
Ermine Street 15
Exeter 17, 60

farming 18–19, *18*, *19*
Fishbourne 42
Forest of Dean 15
fortifications 9, *46*, 47, *53*

forums 8, 17, *44*
Fosse Way 60
freedmen 10–11
freedmen 10–11
funerals 24–5, *25*
Galen 61
Gaul 32, 38, 39, 41, 50, 56, 57, 58
Germanic peoples 56–7, 59
Geta 48–9, *48*
gladiators 17, *17*
glass 14, *15*, *16*, 17
Gloucester 8, 59, 60
gods and goddesses *15*, 19, 21, *21*, 22–3, *22*, *23*, 54, 55
government 8, 26–7, 34–5
governor 26, 34–5, *34*, *35*
Gratian, Emperor 57, 58
Great Witcombe *2–3*, *18–19*

Hadrian, Emperor 16, 46–7, *46*
Hadrian's Wall 7, 10, 21, *21*, 22, 24, *30*, 46–7, *46*, *47*, 49, 54, 61
Herodian 48, 49, 50
High Rochester 37
Hinton St Mary 55
Honorius, Emperor 58
Housesteads 15, 54, *54*
housing 18, *18*, 37. *See also* villas
Hoxne hoard *57*, *59*
hunting 16, *16*
hypocaust *53*

Iceni 42–3, *42*, *43*
Inchtuthil 45
industry 14–15
infantry 27
inhumation 24–5
inns 12, 13
Isis 54

jewellery 6, *36*, *59*
Julia Domna 37, *37*, 48–9, *48*

Lancaster 14
Latin language 45, 60
legal system 60
legionaries 27, *27*, 28–9, *28*, 30, *30*, 31, 45, 47
legionary centurions 27
legionary legates 26–7
Leicester 17, 60
leisure 16–17, *29*
limitanei 53
Lincoln 8, 54
London 8, 9, 8–9, 10, 11, 12, 13, *20*, 25, *25*, 32, 35, *35*, 43, *52*, 54, 55, 56, *56*, 60
Lullingstone *12*, 19, *19*, 22, 55, *55*
Lydney 21

magistrates 8
Maiden Castle 28, 29
Malpas 31, *31*

mansiones 12
manumission 7, 11
Marcus Aurelius, Emperor *23*, 30, *51*
marriage 36, 37
Martial 10, 16
Maryport 31
Massic 33
medicine *14*, 21, 61
merchants 6, 14–15, 27, 38
Mercury 22, *22*, 23, *54*
metal working 14–15, 22
Mildenhall Treasure 55, *55*
mining 14–15
Mithras *22*, 54, *54*, 55
mortaria 15
mosaics 16, *16*, 17, 19, *19*, 25, 53, *53*, 60
Mount Graupius, Battle of 29, 45

Nene Valley 15
Nepos, Platorius 47
Niger 50
Nodens 21
Normans 60

Octavian *see* Augustus, Emperor
Ordovices 44

Patrick, Saint 58
Paullinus 28, 35, 43
Perennis 50
Pertinax 34
Picts 57
Plautius, Aulus 40–1
ploughs *18*
Portchester *51*, *57*
ports 13, *51*, *57*
post-houses 12, 13
pottery 13, 14, *14*, 15, *15*, 17, *17*, 58
Prasutagus 42–3
priests 20–1
primus pilus 27
Priscus 50
procurator 26, *35*

Regina 6–7, *6*
religion *13*, 16, 17, *17*, 19, *19*, 20–3, *20–3*, 53–5, *54*, 55, 59
Richborough *14*, 27, 41, 54, 55, *56*
roads 6, 12–13, *12*, 47, 60
Rudge cup *47*

sacrifice 21, 22, *23*
St Albans 6, 17, 43, 54, 55, 59
Samian ware 15, *15*
Saturnalia 10, 40
Scarborough *57*
Scotland 29, *44*, 45, 48–9, 56–7
senate houses 8
Seneca the Younger 16
Serapis-Osiris 54

Severus, Septimus, Emperor 29, 37, 48–9, *48*, *49*, 50–1, *50*, 52
Severus, Sulpicius 54–5
ships 13, *13*, 15, *39*, 47
shops *14*
Silchester 9, 12, 17, *18*, 53, 55, 60
slavery 6–7, 10–11, *10*, *11*, 24, 43
Snettisham *43*
South Shields 6, *6*
Southwark 9, 54
Suetonius 12, 27, 34, 35, 41, *60*
Sulis 11, 22, 23

Tacitus 8, 9, 11, 18, 20–1, 29, 30, 34, 35, 36, 39, 43, 44, 45
taxation 8, 26, 35
temples 8, 21, *21*, 22–3
Tertullian 54
theatres 8, 17, *17*
Theodosius, Emperor 57
Thracians 6
Tiberius, Emperor 13, *51*
tombstones 6, 7, 11, *24*, 24, 27, *30*, *34*, 35, *35*, *43*, 58
torcs 6, 7, *43*
towns 8–9, 16, 53, 59, *59*
trade 6, 10, 12–13, 14–15, *14*, 18, 38
Trajan, Emperor 27, *29*, 46
Trinovantes 43
Tungrians 32

Uley 22, *22*, 23, 55

Valentinian, Emperor 56
Verecundus, Julius 32
vernae 11
Verulamium *see* St Albans
Vespasian, Emperor 28–9
veterans 8, 27
villas 16, 18, 18–19, *18–19*, 53
Vindolanda 10, 13, 16, 31, 32–3, *32*, *33*, 36, *36*
Virgil 19, 37, *60*
votive objects 23

Wales 44–5, 54
Wall 9, *12*, 13, *17*
Wallbrook 20
wall-paintings 8–9, *36*, *52*, 55
Wallsend 46
Water Newton 15, 55
Weald 15
Wheeldale *12*
Winchester 59
women 36–7, *36*, *37*
Woodchester 53
writing 34, *36*, 61
Wroxeter *4–5*, 8–9, 9, 16, 17, 25, *44*, 58, 59, 60

York 25, 27, 37, 49, *49*, 52, 53, *53*, 54, 60

ACKNOWLEDGEMENTS. **English Heritage would like to thank:**

Dr Christopher Young and Nick Kavanagh for advice; John Banbury, Heather Bird, Paul Birkbeck, Tracey Croft, Peter Connolly, Judith Dobie, Peter Dunn, Derek Lucas, R. Embleton, Jutta Kaiser-Atcherley, Ivan Lapper, Margaret Mahoney, Sue Measer, Joanna Richards and Peter Scholefield for permission to reproduce their illustrations.

The author would like to thank Taylor & Francis for permission to quote from *Roman Britain* by S. Ireland (1986); and Penguin for permission to quote from *Tacitus: The Agricola and the Germania* translated by H. Mattingly and S. A. Handford (1970). He has also made use of the following books: *The People of Roman Britain* by Anthony Birley (Batsford, 1979), *Women in Roman Britain* by Lindsay Allason-Jones (British Museum, 1989), *A History of Roman Britain* by Peter Salway (Oxford, 1993), *Life and Letters on the Roman Frontier* by Alan Bowman (British Museum, 1994) and *The Romanization of Britain* by Martin Millett (Cambridge, 1990).

Picture credits:
(t ch = time chart)
AKG back cover and 14tl, 6cr, 11b, 13b, 25t, 27tl, 37b, 38l, 39t, 39c, 41tl, 44tr, 46, 49c, 50c, 52bl, 53bl, 60bl, 60br; **Ashmolean Museum** 16t; **Augsburg Roman Museum** 12cl;

Bibliothèque Nationale, Paris 61tl; **Bridgeman Art Library** 7tr, 29t, (Archaeological Museum, Naples) cover, (Ashmolean Museum) 38tr, (Fratelli Fabbri, Milan) 48cl, (Giraudon) 58b, (Index) 36l, (National Gallery of Scotland) 20tl, (Private collection) 61r, (State Museum Berlin) 17t, 48t, (The Stapleton Collection) 43c; **British Museum** back cover and 22br, t ch, 54, 10c, 16c, 51b, 18tr, 22tr, 28tl, 31t, 32cl, 35b, 37l, 37t, 38b, 42tl, 43b, 45bl, 54c and t ch, 55b and cover, 59b; **CADW** 31b; **Peter Clayton** 48 and t ch, 34c and map, 37r, 48cr and t ch, 49cr, 50tr, 57b, 30br; **Colchester Museums** 17br, 30t, 43tl and t ch; **Fine Art Photo Library** 42r and t ch; **Fortean Picture Library** 62l; **M. Holford** 10tr, 10bl, 15bl, 20br, 21tr, 22bl, 27t, 34tr, 54t, 55tr, 55tc, 63bl; **Mainz, Landesmuseum** 28c; **Museum of Antiquities, Newcastle-upon-Tyne** 21cl, 47tl, 47tr; **Museum of London** back cover and 28bl, 8bl, 8t, 14b, 20tr, 25br, 34, 35c, 36b, 56tl, 56br; **National Museum of Wales** t ch, 17; **National Museums of Scotland** 44b, 45r; **National Trust** 36b, 53tl; **Osnabrück, Landesmuseum** 29c, 41c; **Scala** 39b and t ch, 11tr, 23t, 26b, 36c, 42b, 50l, 51t; **Trier, Landesmuseum** 19tl, 19br, 35t, 52r; **Tyne and Wear Museums**, Arbeia Fort 6cl, 10tl; **Westfallen Landesbildstelle** 14cr; 24l. All other photographs are the copyright of English Heritage (telephone 0171-973 3338 for details).

Every effort has been made to trace the copyright holders and we apologise in advance for any unintentional omission, which we would be pleased to correct in any subsequent edition of this book.